ORGANIZING INFORMATION

principles and practice

.

ORGANIZING INFORMATION

principles and practice

Christopher Turner

CLIVE BINGLEY 𝒷 LONDON

Published by
Clive Bingley Limited
7 Ridgmount Street
London WC1E 7AE

First published 1987

British Library Cataloguing in Publication Data

Turner, Christopher, *1949–*
   Organizing information : principles and
   practice.
   1. Information services   2. Library
   administration
   I. Title
   020   Z665

   ISBN 0–85157–379–7

Typeset in 10/12 pt Sabon and printed and made in England by Redwood Burn Ltd, Trowbridge, Wiltshire.

Contents

1 An introduction to information units

INFORMATION

Information is the key resource in our society. It is the resource which allows us to change and improve that society; it is the resource which allows economic growth and greater social equality. Traditionally, information has been stored in people's minds and it has been updated and modified through social contact, learning and communication. As society has grown and become more complex, larger quantities of information have been published and disseminated causing an 'information explosion'. At the same time the number of people requiring access to this information has grown dramatically through increased literacy and individuals' realization that the power of information is considerable. However, increasing numbers of people have been deprived of access to information through poverty, illiteracy or lack of knowledge about its importance. Thus, the elderly, the poor, the unemployed and the disadvantaged have been suffering from increased information deprivation.

These two processes – the increasing recognition by many that information is a key resource for social change and, at the same time, an increased deprivation of access to this information – has meant that there is a growing awareness of the importance of information-retrieval systems in the broadest sense. Organizing knowledge through information systems is a vital way of responding to some of the issues involved in information deprivation, the information explosion and the increasing power of information as a social resource.

Libraries and information units have always been key parts of this 'information cycle' (see figure 1) but their commitment has often been towards traditional texts and they have possibly not seen themselves in the role as key elements in economic and social change. It is also true that many members of society have not seen library and

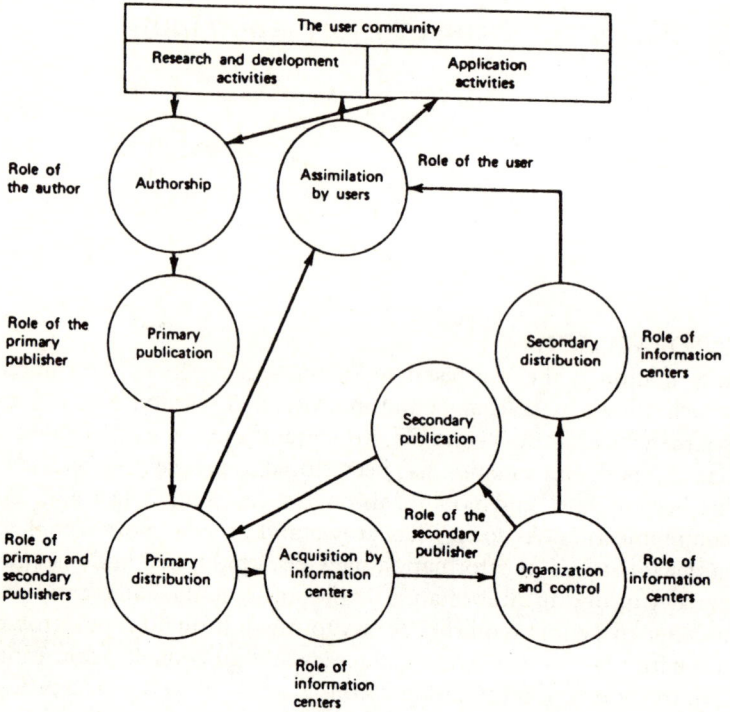

Reproduced with permission from: Lancaster, FW, *Information retrieval systems: characteristics, testing and evaluation.* Wiley, 1979.

1 The information transfer cycle

information units as important sources of the types of information that would allow such change. Thus, research scientists, social workers, businessmen and community counsellors have obtained their information in a very personal ad hoc way involving the principle of least effort. Information is a fairly costly resource to acquire and handle and therefore most individuals prefer to rely on their own personal contacts, personal journals and newspapers. However, the growing impact of the information explosion, the increasing need for rapid social and economic change and the increasing sophistication of information technology and retrieval systems has meant that information units have now become important parts of many advice agencies, research units and research and development centres.

The more traditional role of the library is making way for information units that are actively involved in the relationship of the user with the information system. The rapid growth in specialized information units in areas of community service has been matched by growth of such units in management, business, commerce and scientific research.

Traditional academic, public and special libraries have been very involved in this process of change and have often provided methodologies and processes for the new information services and units. Likewise, the newly emerging information units have fed back into the more traditional libraries an awareness of user interaction, specialized information-retrieval design and, more particularly, the vital importance of information technology with its emphasis on microcomputer applications.

INFORMATION-RETRIEVAL SYSTEMS

Information-retrieval systems involve matching the information needs of users with items that resolve those needs. Traditionally, this meant supplying users with documents, but more recently it has involved providing a far wider range of items including non-print media and access to information on computer databases. It also now involves a far greater awareness of the importance of identifying what users actually do with the information. This often calls for a move into advice, counselling and support roles. Our model of the whole 'information cycle' is therefore far more wide-ranging than was perceived a decade ago.

The information-retrieval model has a number of key stages in it, and this basic guide aims to identify those key stages and provide sufficient information or sources of other information to allow managers of information units to plan and change. Many such units are managed by skilled information scientists and librarians, whilst others are managed by subject experts with less understanding of the basic models of information-retrieval systems. It is for the latter that this guide was primarily produced. The speed of change in some areas, however, and the need to sit back and take a wide overview of the operation of the existing system often means that the trained information scientist or librarian might find a basic guide of this sort useful.

A simple flow diagram of an information-retrieval system can identify the key areas (see figure 2).

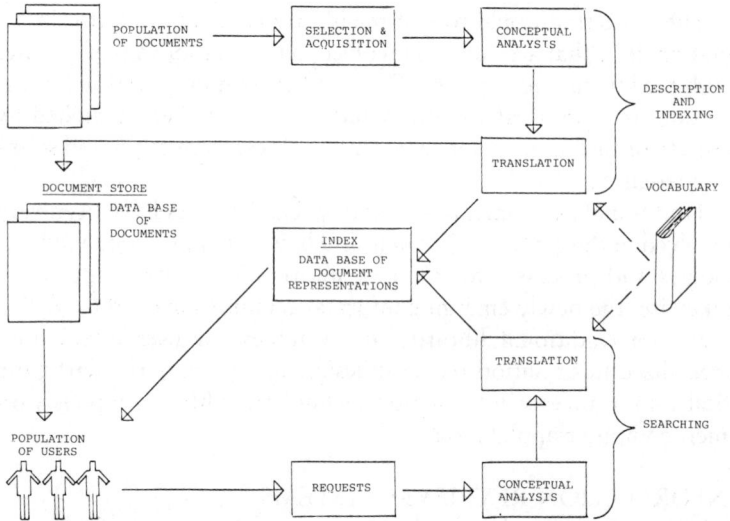

Reproduced with permission from: Lancaster, FW, *Compatibility issues affecting information systems and services*. Paris, Unesco, 1981.

2 **The major components of a typical information service**

The selection and acquisition stage is obviously quite crucial, for without the relevant information in the system all else fails. However the processes of selection and acquisition are outside the specific scope of this guide and are discussed in far greater detail in Alan Bunch's *Basics of information work*. The vital elements of acquiring current and relevant information in a fast and efficient manner, bearing in mind the enormous gaps in information provision and the social and ideological factors which condition the publication of much information, are vital ingredients in the whole information-retrieval process.

The description and indexing subsystem in the information-retrieval model involves the process of identifying what an item is about or what it is trying to say and then describing that in a way which will match the search requirements of the user. This subsystem will require vocabularies or lists of indexing terms, or classification schemes, as well as systems that will allow us to describe precisely the subject content of an item in a consistent and user-oriented fashion.

A major section of this guide discusses the very varied solutions to the problems inherent in the process of describing subject content using real words, artificial words such as classification schemes, or controlled words that allow the indexer and the searcher to agree on what they think the words mean. The very wide range of solutions to some of the problems involved in the description and indexing subsystem suggests that we have an extremely long way to go before total success is achieved and it may well be that the enormously rich and creative role that language plays in society and the way that authors and searchers with highly specific problems use that language in their own very varied fashions mean that information-retrieval systems are always going to be working at a level of second best. Although this can be depressing it can also be exciting in that it means that the very different information-retrieval systems produced across different subject fields and for different users are all sound responses to need, and that change and diversity are continuously being stimulated.

The description and indexing subsystem, although primarily concerned with the subject approach, requires access through many non-subject devices, such as authors, titles, government bodies and organizations and names of other people involved in the item that has to be retrieved. Therefore, as well as discussing indexing vocabularies and indexing systems, this guide will spend some time on basic non-subject approaches that many information units might find useful. There are obviously management implications in the amount of time spent on the subject and non-subject approaches to indexing, and this will be picked up again in a brief section on the choice of systems.

Indexing is a process that enables various surrogates for items to be manipulated in a wide variety of fashions whilst the item itself is retained in some information store or physical arrangement. The description and indexing subsystem therefore produces a wide range of different indexes and catalogues, whilst the information store is arranged using one particular approach depending largely on the type of items in the store. The physical arrangement of the information store is, however, an important part of the retrieval system as many searchers find that browsing or interacting with the actual information itself is far more valuable and creative than having to search through surrogates such as catalogues and indexes. So this guide spends some time discussing the physical arrangement of material, with a particular stress on browsing and physical interaction between the searcher and the information store.

The information-retrieval system has now produced the indexes, catalogues and physical arrangement that allow the user to search the system. The searching subsystem allows the user to structure information needs and present them to the system in a way that will ensure a reasonable match with the information held. However, the searcher has the same problem as the user in terms of defining an information need and then expressing it using the same words as the information-retrieval system. Thus this guide identifies some of the problems in that process and discusses the role of the information officer as an intermediary in that process as well as the importance of a searcher having access to the same vocabulary tools as the indexer.

The output from the retrieval system will obviously vary depending on constraints such as money and time. Some systems that involve the user interacting with the information store itself result in the searcher actually finding answers to problems whilst the search is continuing. However, other systems that involve the user searching surrogates such as catalogues, indexes and on-line databases merely give the user a list of citations or classmarks and accession numbers which then have to be linked to the physical information store. The amount of information given in these surrogates will have some bearing on the user satisfaction with the system and therefore this guide gives some indication about abstracting and descriptive cataloguing of items.

Finally we must recognize that the information-retrieval system is not a closed one. The interaction of the searcher with the information store and the indexes and catalogues must continually modify and change the way those files and stores are structured and arranged. The evaluation process is therefore an important part of the system and a little time is spent on analysing this aspect of the retrieval system. It is also true that the users' interaction with the retrieval system modifies and controls the selection and acquisition stage. Particular users' success stimulates their continued use of the system with the result that the system responds by satisfying these users by acquiring, indexing and then retrieving an increasing amount of relevant information for them. The corollary of this is that the retrieval system might become less relevant to other users who will need to acquire their information elsewhere. This feedback effect is integral to most systems that involve users' choice or preference, and needs to be monitored carefully by the manager of the information unit to ensure that the information-retrieval system is satisfying the information needs of the total population being served rather than the information demands of a small subset.

USERS AND USER NEEDS

Satisfying the information needs of users is the sole function of an information-retrieval system. However, because designing and operating retrieval systems are such intellectually and technically stimulating tasks, it is easy to forget that the individual on the output end of the retrieval system is in fact more important than anything else. It is also true that we know far less about users, user needs and their relationship with information than we do about the more technical, internal aspects of index languages and retrieval systems. This is because it is easier to test, measure and evaluate these internal, technical aspects than it is to study the notoriously difficult area of human interaction.

We need to make a subtle distinction between the user and the end-user or client. Many users of retrieval systems will be information workers, librarians and advice workers who have developed great skill in handling and searching for information within the retrieval system. They have become intermediaries between the information store and the client or person with the technical, social or individual problem that needs to be solved. Thus many end-users may never be actually involved in searching the retrieval system at all. They merely discuss their problems and needs with the skilled intermediary who then does the searching. This intermediary may exist because the technical problems involved in searching the retrieval system are so complex that it would be difficult for the end-user or client to have to learn how to do it for what might be only a very small number of occasions. Continuous interaction with the retrieval system means that the intermediary or information officer becomes highly skilled and specialized and therefore it makes economic sense for the intermediary to be the sole user. Alternatively, in other retrieval systems the client or end-user is also the searcher. This may be because it is preferable for the end-user to be involved in the search in order to have maximum success, or it may be because there are insufficient skilled intermediaries to fulfil this function.

The searching of information-retrieval systems involves a considerable amount of effort. This effort may be physical or mental or both, and this has important implications for the design of systems. A key law of information retrieval was put forward by Mooers as 'an information retrieval system will tend not to be used whenever it is more painful and troublesome for a customer to have information than for him not to have it'. Users will tend to exhaust all personal, local and highly ephemeral information sources before any effort is made to identify and consult more formal sources and centres of information. This means that physical accessibility and ease of use of information centres and information-retrieval systems are of paramount importance. It also means that those users that do make use of information-retrieval systems generally have a high level of need. The cost of not finding the solution to a particular problem is high enough to force the user to go through a process of effort, not least of which is the psychological factor of having to admit to not knowing the answer to a particular problem.

Thus for many information-retrieval systems users are a small group when compared to the total possible population, and non-users of many retrieval systems will outnumber users. This may not matter in some organizations where subject problems are highly technical and specialized and there is a management system which ensures that as soon as one person in the organization knows a particular solution the information is disseminated fairly rapidly; this may happen in the case of scientific and industrial research. However, it becomes far more of a problem when information units are involved in social improvement or community development when a large number of non-users will result in social ignorance about welfare payments, health care or social services support. To reduce the level of non-use, it is often necessary to take management decisions about education programmes, promotion and publicity. Most empirical research however, suggests that at present information is seen as a commodity which has to have very low costs and very high gains before individuals are prepared to make the effort to obtain it.

The success of a particular search in an information-retrieval system will depend on the relationship or interface between the user and the working system. The client has to be able to define a particular information need before anything else can happen. Here lies the nub of the non-user problem, for in many instances this may not be possible. In the same way that a research scientist only identifies a problem when something goes wrong, so an individual may only recognize that a problem exists when a crisis emerges. Thus many information problems in advice centres, for example, are of a crisis nature such as death, unemployment or debt. Even at this stage the definition of need can be very difficult: the problem of debt may be related to long-term poverty which is linked to unclaimed social security benefits.

This expression of demand for information is one of the areas of greatest error in the whole retrieval process. Words may not exist, or the word the client knows does not match the words the retrieval system has used. It is because of this that the majority of initial enquiries tend to be expressed too broadly, with a lack of precision in the terminology used so that the results are wide-ranging and irrelevant.

It is these factors which result in many retrieval systems stressing the importance of the information worker or intermediary helping to improve the user's success. For only an information worker can follow through the range of problems in order to identify the real need of the user for information. The user then becomes an end-user; the intermediary does the searching. However, problems can emerge from this slightly changed relationship. The searcher becomes dependent on the explanation of the problem that is given by the end-user. It is sometimes the case that oral explanations of information problems to the intermediary can be less efficient than a structured letter written at a distance, or personal searching by the client of the retrieval system itself. This is because the intermediary tends to force the client into an expression of an information problem using words and terminologies that already exist within the system. Thus the information unit is constraining the client to present problems in a way that the unit can readily accept.

The problems discussed here are very relevant to the aims and objectives of the information unit, and the ways in which management can plan and lead. The specific problem about the client having difficulty in expressing information needs can be resolved to some extent by well-designed, open-ended enquiry forms. These are completed by each enquirer, with or without the help of the information worker, using the words and terminology of the client, rather than bringing in any of the vocabulary of the information unit at this stage.

Figure 3 gives an example of a case-recording sheet used by the

CLIENT'S PROBLEM	Personal Call Telephone Letter New Repeat *(Please circle)*	Family Name
	Referral From	First Name(s)
		Address
		Telephone No.
		NACAB Categories
		OFT Code Goods/Service Code
YOUR RESPONSE		Letters Drafted
		Phone Calls Made
		Visits to be made
		Referred to
		Worker's Name
		Office Use Only
(Continue on blank sheet if necessary)		Date

Information	Advice	Referral	Counselling	Mediation	Representation	Social Action

MONITORING CODE (Please circle where relevant)

Reproduced with the permission of West Midlands National Association of Citizens' Advice Bureaux.

3 Citizens' Advice Bureaux case-recording sheet

Citizens' Advice Bureaux, but there is a range of alternatives which each information unit must decide on for itself. In the CAB example, multiple-carbon stationery is used so that copies can be filed and an information store built up concerning client demand, arranged by subject and client name. Basic information such as name and address of client, date, information sources consulted, form of communication, etc., can be structured on the form in simple boxes. This allows the maximum space to be used for open-ended statements concerning the information need being expressed. This is entered by the client or information worker using the vocabulary of a client during an interactive discussion of the problem at the beginning of the search.

Users will tend to want particular sorts of response from retrieval systems. They will of course always want the response to be fast, cheap and accurate but such criteria are essentially management aspects and may be impossible to achieve simultaneously! However, within the system itself users will generally require either all the information concerning a particular problem or a specific answer to a specific question. Thus, if the user requires the date of a particular piece of legislation then the first item that gives him that date is all that is needed. Conversely, if a wide-ranging study is being undertaken on the impact of housing benefit on the elderly, a large quantity of data will need to be brought together and the fact that several items all say very similar things does not mean that they should not be consulted. The ability of a retrieval system to satisfy these differing sorts of demand is judged through the two measures of recall and precision.

Recall is the ability of a retrieval system to obtain all or most of the relevant items in the system. Thus if there are 80 relevant items known to exist in the system and the user manages to obtain 40 of them through searching in the index, the system has achieved a 50% recall ratio.

At the same time a user does not want to retrieve rubbish, or 'noise'. Each individual search will throw up a number of items, some of which are relevant and some of which are not. A search may produce ten items, of which seven are relevant and three irrelevant. Such a search would have a precision ratio of 70%. Thus precision is a measure of irrelevance or 'noise', or the amount of work that a user has to do in order to sift through all of the items retrieved to find those that are specifically relevant.

Particular levels of recall and precision are the result of different types of index language, differing levels of detail in the indexing process and the problem of agreeing on what is relevant. Much of this guide is concerned with these particular aspects.

TYPES OF MATERIAL

The problems of organizing information, especially from a subject point of view, are obviously related to the subjects content of items rather than to the types of material or formats. Thus there are many more difficulties with language, meaning, structures of terms and relationships in the design of retrieval systems than there are with the physical differences between a pamphlet, a book and a client's case-record. In fact retrieval systems tend to take the view that the subject content and concepts, and the ways that searchers respond to them, are far more similar across various physical forms of material than they are different. One of the great arguments in favour of catalogues and similar retrieval tools is that they enable the information unit to bring together at one place all the available information that might be scattered by the various forms in which the information was originally acquired.

However, it is clear that the process of physically interacting with the information within a unit is probably one of the most creative information-retrieval systems available. This ability to browse in the information store, be it books on shelves or files in a cabinet, using a backwards-and-forwards, question-and-answer technique whereby the user slowly narrows down the half-formulated inquiry to the specific problem that requires an answer, formally called an heuristic process, is an activity that many retrieval systems are striving to achieve.

This physical interaction is less possible with computerized retrieval systems, and much of the interest in what are termed expert systems is in the possibility that this heuristic question-and-answer process can be built into computerized retrieval systems.

Although the physical form of material should not make any impact on the effectiveness of retrieval systems, in reality the success that an individual client might have from a system could be very dependent on the physical format of information within that system. Books and similar text-bearing artifacts are specifically designed for browsing and an heuristic process of identifying relevance. Thus the cover, title page, contents list and chapter headings are all devices that allow the searcher to identify the precise level of relevance of the item. Book-based information systems will therefore tend to have a high level of user satisfaction from broad-based browsing arrangements. Alternatively, information-bearing artefacts such as films, audio recordings and similar are inefficient in terms of identifying relevance and allowing browsing. The ability to lift out one particular piece of information from the middle of a video is extraordinarily difficult when compared to the ability to do the same with a monograph or periodical article.

Thus the design of our retrieval system must take into account the ability of the items to assist and stimulate the information-retrieval process or bar and reduce the process. This point is not a particularly sophisticated one, but it needs to be recognized by the designer of the information-retrieval system. There is always a possibility that we will spend too much of our time concerning ourselves with indexing simple items that users may have few problems with, at the expense of those items that present enormous difficulties to them. It is also possible that our decision to do this may be related to the same sort of problems that users have! Thus, detailed indexing and retrieval systems for material such as films or videos, slides or audio tapes, ephemeral community information and local authority committee meeting minutes are not as abundant or sophisticated as some of the subject-retrieval systems that have been designed for books. This is because it is extremely difficult to analyse much of the difficult material into subject-based concepts that can then be input into our retrieval system.

We can identify a range of materials that will exist within information units and advice centres, covering a continuum from the traditional book containing information-bearing text through to a video-recording with no text and possibly very little hard information. This continuum will include periodicals, conference proceedings, government reports, local authority reports, and a large group of text-bearing artifacts which are difficult to handle, such as single sheet handouts, clippings from newspapers and sections of committee minutes. Traditional librarians have a strong interest in the text-based format, but are rapidly improving their abilities to handle the non-text materials. Information workers in advice centres and similar units have always had a strong involvement in the more ephemeral groups of text-bearing information, such as fact sheets, bulletins and similar.

The need for information units to identify gaps in the information provision and to attempt to fill those gaps by producing their own information-dissemination tools has led to a growing interest in the information unit as a producer of information. The National Association of Citizens' Advice Bureaux information department, for example, has always been in the business of formatting and repackaging information into a structure which is more easily handled by hard-pressed voluntary advice-workers. Librarians have possibly been less involved in this process, but more specialist subject library and information units such as Help For Health have recently been filling gaps in the information provision of text-based formats.

The impact of new technology will make a difference in this area. Word-processing, electronic publishing, Prestel, cheap video and tape-slides formats are all very powerful methods of allowing gaps in the traditional information flow to be filled. The cost of access to many of the new technologies is decreasing rapidly; domestic video equipment and microcomputers with word-processing facilities are obvious examples of technology that in a short space of time have come down to reasonable prices. The result is that community information systems and advice agencies are now fully able to produce text- or video-based information packages on issues of interest in a very short space of time. Around the country there are examples of both local community video projects and information data bases being produced. The merging of the two through interactive video, whereby microcomputers can control video formats in a sophisticated education and learning process, is still very expensive but experience suggests that such costs may well come tumbling down.

These trends suggest that information systems will soon need to become very involved in handling a wide range of formats that are at present outside their thinking. The emergence of such a wide range of differing formats is bound to have some implications for the design of retrieval systems and the organization of information. These implications may be simply on the level of physical arrangement and display, but they will also impinge on cataloguing and the description of items as well as raise some difficulties over conceptualizing what things are actually 'about'. We are able to look at a periodical or a pamphlet and specify with some reasonable agreement what the author is primarily trying to say. We can then match some of the words used in the item against the words used in our retrieval systems and recognize that this item is saying the same sort of thing as some other item and therefore ensure the system links the two together through either a classmark or a subject heading. This process becomes more difficult when we move into the areas of film, video and possibly audio. The matching process is more difficult, and the greater power of visual imagery means that agreement on what the author is trying to say might be more difficult. Thus, a locally-produced video charting the decline of the old working-class regions and the emergence of new council-house estates can be difficult to handle unless we keep very clear in our mind the exact function of our retrieval system.

THE ARRANGEMENT OF MATERIALS

The physical arrangement of items is the primary retrieval method in many information-storage and retrieval systems. It is by using the physical arrangement that searchers and end-users actually find most of the information that they need. It is obviously more useful and relevant for searchers to move through the information store handling the items and looking at them in order to identify the particular solution to the problem. Many library and information units have been more concerned with back-up and support indexes to the physical arrangement of items, without recognizing the crucial nature of this initial physical arrangement.

Browsing and information retrieval

The process by which searchers narrow down and identify the items that are of relevance to them is important. We have already recognized that many searchers are not precisely aware of what they need or want. This can be true for both the end-user and the intermediary, either information officer, librarian or advice worker. An activity that is heuristic in nature has to take place. This simply means that the searcher identifies the real need through a series of implicit questions to the system, with each answer allowing the searcher to define the need more precisely. Thus, a broad problem of welfare rights is narrowed down to specific benefit entitlements by looking at items in the system and by following up those that are relevant, recognizing that there is a particular problem to do with the non-claiming of housing benefit.

This heuristic dialogue will often take place between a searcher and a client before the system is approached, but very often the searcher will also need the heuristic feedback that the system itself provides in order to identify the specific need of a client. Similarly, the client may be doing the searching and therefore the feedback mechanism becomes even more important.

Thus we can see that the physical arrangement of items in the retrieval system is an integral part of the whole searching process, and needs to be planned with care. The contexts within which a particular item is arranged may stimulate and spark off new lines of enquiry, and the manager of the information unit may need to make use of this when designing a retrieval system to help users of the retrieval system to find all the important relevant information.

The concept of an heuristic search process is tied in with the idea of browsing. Although this term conjures up the idea of aimless drifting through a retrieval system, the recognition of the heuristic process means that if searchers are only very broadly aware of their needs then a broad browse through the part of the system that seems most relevant may be the only way of narrowing down the need to a specific solution. Thus browsing allows some degree of user interaction with the whole collection, or a large part of it, and stimulates retrieval of the half-sought or totally unknown items. Recognition of the importance of browsing may not lead us to any specific arrangement of material, but indicates the importance of subject groupings and physical arrangements which allow or even force searchers to look at items in the system.

Surveys have indicated a surprisingly high level of serendipity or chance retrieval in this process. By this we mean the purely random process of identifying items that might be relevant for future need or were relevant to a problem that was identified in the past. The importance of serendipity is purely that it reinforces the need for a retrieval process which forces searchers to get to know as intimately as possible items in the system. For very large retrieval systems such as international on-line databases this is obviously out of the question, but for small units with collections that are intimately related to the specific needs of users such a plan is important.

Traditional arrangements of libraries

The arrangement of materials in libraries is generally based on subject grouping of books in a fashion that stimulates and even forces browsing. This subject grouping on the shelves normally follows one of the major bibliographic classification schemes. General libraries, such as academic libraries and public libraries that cover all subject fields, might follow the decimal classification of Melvil Dewey or the Library of Congress classification. In more specialist units the collection might be arranged by one of the multiplicity of specialist subject classifications or by the Universal decimal classification.

These bibliographic classification schemes were originally designed primarily for the arrangement of books on shelves. However, pressure on them to become information-retrieval tools with highly detailed subject approaches and very specific terminology has resulted in some conflicts. Greater specificity of terminology will result in more detailed, and therefore longer, classmarks. The increased specificity will also produce an arrangement in which there are a greater number of more precise subject groupings, each with far fewer items in them. This is obviously advantageous for the user with known subject requirements, but can result in a reduction in chance gains from browsing and may even reduce the stimulus to browsing that such arrangements are primarily designed for.

We shall look at the specific subject-based classification schemes in another section, and will discuss in some detail the major advantages and disadvantages of a range of different classification schemes.

BROAD SUBJECT ARRANGEMENTS

Many libraries have been concerned at the problems involved in using the traditional bibliographic classification schemes for their arrangement, and have identified alternatives. 'Traditional classification schemes, in creating a logical set of relationships between subjects, fail to take account of the changing interests which lead people to approach those subjects' (Betts). This concern relates to the datedness, academic structure and general bias towards certain user groups of the general classification schemes. There is also the worry that the major bibliographic classification schemes have become large and unwieldy, with a notation that is too complex and is not allocated to ensure that the most important subject areas are treated in the greatest detail.

The alternative as seen by many libraries is to produce a classification scheme that matches the needs of the user in terms of the physical arrangement of stock. Many libraries call this process 'stock categorization', but in reality it is a return to designing a broad-based classification scheme that meets the needs of the library's user group. The traditional bibliographic classification schemes started in this fashion themselves, and then grew as the demands of libraries and documents changed.

This move toward broad subject groupings in the generalist libraries is a move that many small information units at the beginning of their development may want to copy. Within the broad subject groupings, anything from 12–90 categories (see figure 4 for an example), items are arranged by either author or title or possibly randomly.

Broad subject categories are effectively main-class arrangements that stimulate or force browsing and so produce a high level of recall. Because searchers are made to scan all the items within the broad subject grouping to find a specific subject item that is required, they will generally find something that is relevant. Thus a number of specific items on different aspects of canals might be in a broad category of transport. All items in the category will have to be scanned to retrieve the various items on canals, ensuring in the process that the searcher has looked at virtually every item on canals in the system.

This approach is an excellent example of a high-recall retrieval system achieved at minimal cost. The disadvantage of this sytem is borne by the user who does require a specific item and is forced to spend a great deal of time browsing to retrieve this known item.

Broad-based systems in specialist information units

This broad subject approach, although only recently popular in public libraries (see Ainley and Totterdell), has always been of great interest and value in small information units. The pressure of large quantities of ephemeral information, the lack of staff, the lack of time, and the uncertainty over the detailed structure of the rapidly changing subject field has resulted in information units, in the advice world particularly, using broad-based categories for the physical arrangement of their materials.

The ephemeral nature of the items – pamphlets, single sheets or handouts – results in physical handling problems as well as great uncertainty over what an item is actually 'about'. Systems respond by using filing cabinets or large boxes, which can best be arranged

LIST OF CATEGORIES FOR SMALL/MEDIUM LIBRARIES
(10,000–30,000 VOLUMES)

A SCIENCE
General Science
Mathematics
Physics
Chemistry
Biology
Astronomy

B COUNTRYSIDE AND ANIMALS
Pets
Wildlife
Countryside

C HOME
Gardening
Cooking
Do It Yourself
Car Maintenance
Health
Etiquette

D LEISURE
Collecting
Hobbies
Sports
Handicrafts

E ENTERTAINMENT
Music
Theatre
Cinema
Dance
Humour
The Media

G ART
Art History
Architecture

H LITERATURE
Literary Criticism
Poetry
Plays

K LANGUAGES

L HOLIDAYS
Guide·Books
Camping
Caravanning

M TRAVEL

N HISTORY
History
Local Studies

P BIOGRAPHY

Q GENERAL READING
Fiction
Non-fiction

R HISTORICAL NOVELS

S ROMANCES

T ADVENTURE
Adventure
Sea Stories
Westerns
Science Fiction

U WAR
Militaria
War

V CRIME

W THE UNKNOWN
The Unknown
Ghosts
Witchcraft
Horror
Astrology

X SOCIETY
Religion
Education
Sociology
Citizens Rights

Y TRANSPORT
Road
Rail
Air
Water

Z PEOPLE AT WORK
Careers
Management
The Office
Industrial Relations

LP LARGE PRINT

Reproduced with the permission of East Sussex County Library.

4. Example of a list of categories for small/medium libraries (10,000–30,000 volumes)

using broad subject categories that relate to the needs of the users of the system. Subject categories such as:

Debt
Housing
Unemployment

have been used by many small advice agencies. As collections grow, new categories emerge or decline and this will require continuous change in the categories. Initially, the categories will change and be modified fairly frequently as the unit makes decisions about the headings it will need to use. After a period the workers will find a structure that maximizes user satisfaction and minimizes problems. All such solutions will have to be 'second best' in that an arrangement will always inconvenience a particular subject approach by scattering related materials, but the key will be to identify the initial range of characteristics of the subject that the user will find most useful.

Once the breakdown into broad headings has been produced and the groupings that are to be used have been identified, decisions will need to be made about what items go into which category or heading. Many items will contain information on several of the categories. Debt and housing may be discussed in the same pamphlet. Pragmatic solutions will emerge in that information workers will be able to rank the various categories and put debt above housing, or vice versa, for their particular information requirements.

Thus a list of broad subject categories emerges – marriage, health, housing, debt, etc. – with some explicit rules about which items go into which categories when several exist in the same item. If marriage and debt are discussed in a pamphlet it might be agreed that debt is so important that all items on debt must come together, even if it means separating some of the information on marriage. All items on marriage alone will of course be collected in the file for marriage.

What emerges is a mechanism for grouping material into subject categories that match user needs, along with some simple decisions about ranking of the subjects to allow a choice to be made when there are items that cover several categories. This is an embryonic classification scheme for information retrieval, and if designed well initially can be expanded and developed to meet growing and changing requirements.

As a next stage, the broad categories can be assigned numbers, or notation, and the numbers can be linked together to indicate that an item is about both housing and debt while allowing it to be filed at the place for the more important concept of the two. With such a development the system moves from a broad system of ordering to what is known as an analytico-synthetic classification scheme. In such schemes items are analysed for content and the numbers indicating that content are brought together, or synthesized, to form a classmark showing the full subject specification of the item. Such an approach is discussed more fully in Chapter 3.

How to produce a broad subject arrangement

An information unit can produce such a broad system of arrangement relatively easily. The decisions need to be a mixture of discussions with staff and users, along with an analysis of the materials in the system. Discussions with searchers will need to identify:

a) the broad groups that users think they are searching for when they come into the system. Specific terms such as housing or debt or immigration need to be discussed with searchers to identify their response to such groupings.

b) The ranking that searchers put to the concepts that need to be identified. Do searchers feel that debt is more important than housing, or do they prefer an even broader approach?

The material in the system will need to be analysed to see if broad groupings are inherent within the collection. Analysis of the material should indicate:

a) The possibility of broad groupings based on users' problems, such as debt or unemployment; or groupings based on agencies, such as hospitals or social services.

b) The need to have broad categories for 'processes' such as tactics. The alternative to having such categories would be to put tactics on a particular problem with the problem itself.

From this process it should be possible to identify for a small information unit with a collection of material that is just being brought together a grouping of some 12 to 20 subject categories into which the material can be grouped. These subject categories can be used to label boxes or filing cabinets into which all material is rapidly filed when it comes into the unit. Such a broad subject grouping may not be the long-term solution for the storage and retrieval of information within the unit, but it is a good practical solution to designing a retrieval system in the early stages of development of a unit, and it ensures that the unit is not dragged into using traditional bibliographic classification schemes in the mistaken belief that they will work. Once the grouping of broad subject categories has been agreed upon by information workers within the system, they can be typed out and posted on walls and used in bulletins and handouts. However, it is important to realize that these grouping will not remain constant for long. New user demands and new forms of material will force a re-think on the categories at fairly regular intervals.

The major element in forcing a re-think on categories will be the searchers. Their constant interaction with the collection and its arrangement should throw up ideas on alternative methods of grouping and more sophisticated ways of sub-arranging within each of the categories. It is important that the searchers in the system are able to modify the subject categories, and that the searching and subject-categorizing process do not become divorced. Of course, any changes in the categories will mean that a re-indexing of the materials has to take place. Thus, each time a new category is decided on, or there is a change in existing categories, all the relevant information has to be taken out of the system and re-assigned to the new categories. It is this re-indexing process that stops changes and modifications taking place too frequently. It is also a strong incentive to make sure that the categories decided upon at the beginning, after discussion with staff and clients, are as valuable and relevant as possible.

PHYSICAL FORMS OF STORAGE

Although the physical form of the storage of materials in information units should theoretically have no effect on the efficiency of the retrieval system, it is obvious that certain methods of storage and arrangement will stimulate and assist searchers. As the importance of browsing and physical searching through the information unit is now clear, any storage mechanism that stimulates this process is to be preferred. As a rule of thumb, therefore, any storage mechanism that reduces searchers' abilities to handle the items as they are searching is to be avoided. Thus as we run through some of the main forms of material that we might find in the information units, we can see the sort of storage devices that will be useful.

Books. There is very little that needs to be said about storing books on shelves. The whole publication and physical layout of a book is designed on the assumption that it will be stored and filed on a shelf, generally using the author's name as a sub-filing mechanism within a broad subject arrangement.

Pamphlets. The great difficulty here is in deciding whether a pamphlet is akin to a book, and therefore should be stored on a shelf with books, or whether it is a format that is better arranged with the more ephemeral physical formats such as handouts and single-sheet documents in a hanging filing system. A sensible pragmatic response might be to decide which of the two storage mechanisms is more used inside the unit, and then put pamphlets in that system. Thus, if books are the main form of material then pamphlets should go with books. If ephemeral literature stored in files is the main source of information, then pamphlets should go there. A sensible cut-off point regarding the size of the pamphlet could probably be whether the title and author were on the spine of the pamphlet, in which case it would be regarded as a book. The major danger here is that pamphlets, a very vital information source within most units, might be lost if stored in the wrong place.

Information sheets, handouts and ephemera. In a large number of information units these sources of information are the lifeblood of the system. As always, our response must be to try and store them in a way that ensures searchers have physical contact with the information if possible. Thus lateral filing-cabinets, which tend to reduce browsing, are to be rejected in favour of vertical filing-cabinets which although not perfect at least allow files to be lifted out and the information in them scanned through. Within the vertical filing cabinet, open-pocket wallets are to be preferred because they allow a whole drawer to be scanned through quickly, whilst closed wallets with flaps force a searcher to lift out, open and look through each file in turn. Open folders with treasury tags also allow the file to be opened on the desk and searched through, possibly with a client or end-user to assist the final choice.

Multimedia formats. These are extremely difficult to arrange in a fashion that stimulates or even allows any sort of browsing. By definition video-tapes and audio-recordings cannot be scanned in the normal fashion and therefore the packaging and displaying become vital. Commercially produced video-tapes can be arranged like

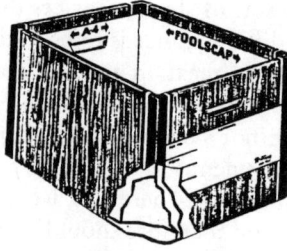

5 'R-kive' storage box, showing strong construction

books, for they normally have information-bearing packaging. However, internally produced video-tapes or recordings often lack any eye-catching information. The same applies to audio-tapes, and in both cases bold, home-produced graphics are probably far better than the neatly typed labels which are one's normal response to such arrangements.

Shelves and filing cabinets can be very expensive if the information unit is being set up from scratch. The use of 'R-kive' storage boxes (figure 5) can be useful. They are stout boxes with lids, which can be used as vertical filing-boxes or simply left open with piles of ephemeral documentation inside so that searchers can browse; broad subject headings can be assigned to each box. They can also be placed on their sides so that they can be used for the storing and arranging of books or videos.

2 Catalogues and cataloguing

THE NEED FOR CATALOGUES AND INDEXES

If the physical arrangement of the items in the system matches the retrieval demands of the user then there are few worries over the alternative ways users need to retrieve information. Thus if all user demands are for subjects that match the subject arrangement chosen, or all demands are for the report numbers by which items are arranged, the cost-effectiveness of providing alternative approaches is zero.

However, it is unusual for physical arrangement to be quite so satisfactory. Whatever arrangement we produce it can follow only one particular chosen order: subject, author or some other alternative. In many cases there will be demands for access points to items through other aspects: author, title, report number or subject; or it might be necessary to provide access through subjects that were regarded as less important when categories were ranked. It is for these alternative approaches that catalogues or indexes need to be produced.

The decision on the cost-effectiveness of alternative access points through catalogues is an important one, for the extra effort involved in providing them can be large. We will need to analyse the extra tasks involved so that reasonable decisions on cost-effectiveness can be made.

a) An item will need to be analysed in greater detail in terms of its subject, author, title and any other access points that might be relevant. This process of analysis will take longer than the basic decision over what the item is mainly about and for what it will normally be used. However, the increased time spent on this analysis may be marginal. Every item must be analysed in order to come up with the first decision, and therefore the subsequent analysis may take only a few more minutes.

b) Obviously not every item will have to have access points under every possible approach. Therefore a decision will need to be made over which access points will and will not be provided.

c) The extra access points will need to be turned into a catalogue or index. This will involve physical production of catalogue cards, strips, loose leaf slips or a database. The physical form of such catalogues will be discussed later in this chapter, but they will all involve some sort of inputting process, whether it be typing, handwriting or entering into a microcomputer.

d) The physical entries will then need to be filed into whatever cataloguing system is chosen. In the case of small microcomputers this filing process will be an automatic spin-off from the software. However, in the case of manual systems such as index cards or slips this filing process can be extraordinarily expensive in terms of staff time. There are undoubted advantages of such a filing process, in that it makes searchers or information workers aware of the spread of information within the system and the way that the retrieval system works. However, its cost is high when it is remembered that these are supplementary access points, and that during the short lifetime of a piece of ephemeral information none of the access points might be used at all.

Careful analyses of the way searchers approach the information store will yield information on whether or not provision of such back-up catalogues and indexes is worth considering. Searchers and end-users will be able to identify the number of times that access to documents through authors, particularly corporate authors and government departments, titles and report numbers, etc., are required. From this it is possible to make judgements on the importance of such access points.

Libraries have traditionally regarded the provision of alternative access points as a fundamental task in organizing the information within a large working system. Much of their experience has been in handling material that is to be used over reasonably long periods of time and which is often sought through access points such as author and title. Libraries are also normally fairly large, and therefore the importance of the catalogue in locating items as well as informing a searcher as to whether an item exists is important. Not all of these conditions will apply, however, in small information units.

The use of microcomputers has transformed the process of producing alternative access points. Software packages ensure that a single process of inputting a standard block of information about each item can result in the production of indexes and arrangements by a wide variety of alternative access points.

AUTHOR-TITLE CATALOGUES

Catalogues and indexes are retrieval tools that support the physical arrangement of the information by providing alternative access points in different sequences.

Catalogues contain reasonably full information about each item, sufficient to choose and identify it. Indexes merely provide a number or some other locational device. Indexes are normally subject tools which lead from subject access points to whatever it is that is used to arrange the information – a page number in a book, a classmark, or a report number. The distinction between an index and a catalogue is often blurred, and the two terms are often used synonymously.

Catalogues and indexes can be arranged by author's name, title, report number or a wide range of subject arrangements that duplicate and augment the physical arrangement of items.

Catalogues can be broken into two major groups: those that are for access through the subject approach (which will be dealt with later in this guide) and those that provide access through other identifiers such as author, title, report number, etc.

Functions of author-title catalogues

The functions of author-title catalogues are fairly self-evident:

a) The catalogue identifies whether an item exists in the system that has been written by a particular person or corporate body, or has a particular title, or has a particular report number, etc.
b) The catalogue also locates a particular item by showing a piece of notation or giving a location number that allows the item to be physically retrieved.

These two functions, of identifying and of locating, would normally happen at one and the same time, by the provision of information under each access point showing where in the system each item is physically stored. The importance of this is that, as we have already recognized, our physical arrangement will often require a number of sequences, depending on whether the materials are books, pamphlets, ephemera, etc. The catalogue will allow all these different physical sequences to be brought together and be searched as if they were one single sequence.

A third function of catalogues is to allow searchers to choose items they require without having to find the specific items themselves. This function tends to maximize searchers' time by giving information on particular items that will allow them to be discarded or chosen before the physical arrangement itself has to be consulted. Information on date, the language of the item, its length, its contents or possibly its importance or bias are all factors that will allow the searcher to reject certain items and therefore reduce time spent in locating them in the physical arrangement of materials. As systems become larger this choice function may become more and more important. It may also be particularly important when the actual items cannot be browsed through easily, such as video-films or slides. However, when items are easily found and exist in simple, single-sequence arrangements, the amount of information required to assist this choice factor can often be kept to a minimum.

Elements of author-title cataloguing

Searching under authors' names, whether personal or of corporate bodies such as government departments and institutions, is one of the most valuable ways of discovering quickly whether an item exists in an information unit and where it is located. The person or corporate body responsible is an identifier that allows the searcher to produce rapidly a usable subset from a very large information store – provided the person or body responsible for the document is known in the first place. Hence the author approach is designed for the cognoscenti; it assumes some level of reasonable knowledge, acquired through lists, personal contacts or previous reading.

The use of authors' names as access points to systems has had a long history in the academic world – of which librarians are normally a part. It has taken time for librarians to recognize that authors' names are not always as valuable as titles or subjects for many users. However, the author approach in the majority of libraries and information units is still extraordinarily useful, and therefore a detailed discussion of the problems is necessary here.

Main entry

Librarians have traditionally regarded the author as the main entry point for users into catalogues and retrieval systems and it was here that the fullest record was provided. This idea of the main entry was once all-important, particularly when the author approach was the only form of access provided by catalogues. The ease of production of catalogues that provide multiple access points such as cards, but more especially those based on microcomputers, has meant that the concept of a main entry has reduced in importance. Many catalogues now merely repeat the same amount of information about the item under as many different names of authors, organizations, editors, or titles as are felt to be reasonable access points by a user to that particular item. This obviously simplifies some of the decisions involved in cataloguing, and requires a series of fairly basic decisions about how many access points can be afforded for each item.

However, there is obviously a need for some single recognized identifier which can be used to search for an item in bibliographies, international databases and any other listings that require references to particular documents. This need for a single identifier means that the concept of a main entry heading is often still important. There are also still catalogues that can only afford to have one entry made in them. For such catalogues the decision over which is the single main identifier becomes important.

This decision on the main entry or heading for an item is based on the concept of intellectual responsibility.

Intellectual responsibility

The main entry, or key access point, for a document will be under the person or group primarily responsible for the intellectual content of the item. Thus authors' names are used as the headings for their books, composers' names are the headings for their music, photographers' names are the headings for collections of their photographs. This principle allows books, journal articles, research reports, most non-book formats including a reasonable proportion of audio and visual material such as videos, sound-recordings and films to be entered readily in catalogues. If a group of people have produced the work then the corporate name of the group is used as the heading, and if there is no name of a person intellectually responsible the work is entered under title.

This statement of the general principle of intellectual responsibility has obviously glossed over specific problems that will occur in cataloguing some items, but the general concept is sound and should be referred back to whenever doubt arises.

Added entries
The idea of a main entry implies that catalogues will also be full of a wide range of added entries. These added entries are headed by all the names of individuals and groups who are not primarily responsible for the existence of the work but who are inextricably linked to that work. This will include the names of editors, illustrators, translators, chairmen of reports, many different forms of corporate body and any other name that a user of the catalogue might search for.

If in doubt about added entries, always make one. The only constraint will be the costs of producing extra copies of the catalogue entry and the cost of filing the increased number of entries. Therefore a simple cost-effective trade-off needs to be made between the likelihood of a user requiring that access point and the cost of providing it. Obviously access to computer-produced catalogues, whether micro or mainframe, means that the marginal cost of producing extra entries is extremely low and as many added entries as the user might think of can be made. Low-budget manual systems, however, would have to consider very carefully the fairly high increased cost involved in providing a multiplicity of added entries.

The simple principle of intellectual responsibility and multiple added entries must not obscure the fact that there will still be some fairly complicated decisions to be made over headings and added entries in some of the items that will be acquired for the information unit. In order to assist in some of these decisions there are sets of cataloguing rules that librarians have produced as international standards. These will be discussed later in this chapter. However, the basic idea that we are producing catalogues in order to help users gain access to information should allow us to solve most problems about what access points need to be provided in catalogues.

Forms of Name for Headings
There is a second group of problems involved in providing author-title catalogues. These are decisions about the forms of name that need to be used in the catalogue for authors, corporate bodies, titles or any other names that might be reasonably sought by the user. These difficulties over variant forms of name are a jungle of conflicting problems, which can result in a user entering the system with a precise name and being unable to link it with the item in the system.

The main and added entries in catalogues will result in three different forms of name. Firstly there will be all the personal names of individuals involved with any of the items in the system. Secondly there will be all the corporate bodies, including government departments, institutions and other organizations that are in any way responsible for the content of the work. Thirdly there will be the titles of reports, monographs and books, films, series, pamphlets, etc., which have been entered in the system either as added entries or main entries.

People

Most people have a recognizable surname and some sort of forename. For ease of filing and general usefulness headings for such people are simply their surnames followed by their forenames. However, a number of interesting difficulties emerge in this area.

An individual may have more than one name. Popes, kings and noblemen all have a variety of legitimate names. Actors, politicians, writers, married people, divorced people may all have several names. A simple working principle to solve this group of problems is to adopt the name by which the person is commonly known in the literature or in reference sources and other books. Thus we shall have headings such as **Benn, Tony; Pope John the 23rd; Carter, Jimmy** and **Hope, Bob.**

The individual has only one name but it is in several distinct parts or a format which is unlike the normal surname and forename. This group of problems includes compound surnames such as double-barrelled or hyphenated surnames, prefixes, titles of nobility and similar. Names such as **Walter de la Mare, Charles de Gaulle, Patrick Gordon-Walker,** and **John Foster-Dulles** are all in this group. The general principle behind solving most of these difficulties is to accept the name as it stands most of the time. Thus hyphenated names and compound surnames are used without modification, as are most prefixes, resulting in headings such as **de la Mare, Walter.** Exceptions to this are certain foreign prefixes such as **de** in French and **Von** and **Van** in German when the prefix is ignored and the surname following the prefix is used as the entry point. This is because those prefixes are used so often they become absurd as access points. Forms of names such as titles of nobility are allowed as headings as long as they are normally used by the author.

An important factor here, as in most other cataloguing problems is to maintain a high level of consistency. Many of these problems with the forms of name have no correct solutions and the catalogue merely attempts to mirror the normal approach of the user. The educative process of using the catalogue is such that once a principle of searching under, for example, prefixes is accepted then the user will be able to follow that principle when a similar problem occurs at a future time.

A key element in this educative process is the use of references. Whenever there is a decision about any form of name problem, whether for individuals or corporate bodies, then references must always be made from the variant forms of name which have not been chosen. These references lead the user to the name that has been chosen. Thus, if **de la Mare, Walter** is the accepted entry form then there must be references that read **Mare, Walter de la** *see* **de la Mare, Walter** and **la Mare, Walter de** *see* **de la Mare, Walter**. These two separate references will file in the catalogue under **Mare** and **la Mare** and allow the user to be led to the correct place. That process of leading the user will also be an educative one and each searcher will identify the simple principles at work.

Corporate bodies

There is also a range of separate difficulties involved in corporate or institutional names. As before the solution to most of these problems will, as far as possible, be a sensible pragmatic response which will match the particular requirements of the user. Again, references will always have to be made from all the variant forms of name that have not been accepted leading to the form of name that is used as a heading. As with personal names, most corporate bodies and institutions have a single name which is recognizable and identifiable. This results in headings such as **British Broadcasting Corporation** and **Milk Marketing Board**. However, problems do arise and they can be grouped into a number of categories.

A body can have a number of different names. This can happen because of different languages or names changing over time. The pragmatic solution to this difficulty will be to use the form of name adopted by the corporate body itself in their publications, or alternatively the form of name used in normal reference sources. This will mean that as names of institutions change over time different headings will be produced in the catalogue. Items might therefore be entered under **London County Council** as well as **Greater London**

Council, depending on when the item was published. There must obviously be references leading across from each heading to the other heading. Thus: **London County Council** *see also the later heading* **Greater London Council;** **Greater London Council** *see also the earlier heading* **London County Council.**

Many corporate bodies are subordinate to some larger parent organization. This causes some conflict in deciding whether an item is to be entered under the name of the subordinate body or the name of the parent body. For example, the Bodleian Library is part of Oxford University. How is the heading to be entered? Again we respond pragmatically. All subordinate bodies can be entered directly under their own name unless:

a) Its name is not individual enough to identify it specifically, or the name of the parent body is part of the name of the subordinate body;

b) It is a subordinate body that is created or controlled by a government, in which case the heading is the heading for the government itself.

Problems of uniqueness of name are fairly simple, with a solution which allows the cataloguer to enter a work under the name of the corporate body that appears on the title page of the document unless the heading that results is not sufficiently unique. Thus **the Bodleian Library** is entered under **Bodleian Library,** but a heading such as **School of Pharmacy** has to be entered under the parent body to give **London University. School of Pharmacy.** Similarly, **the Photographic Society of Brighton Polytechnic** is entered as **Brighton Polytechnic. Photographic Society.**

The second group of problems to do with government departments is, however, inherently rather more complex, because government departments are major producers of information sources and their structure and interrelationships often seem cumbersome and unwieldy.

Corporate bodies that are part of central or local government are entered under the heading for the government or local authority, and this heading is the geographical name of the area being governed. The logic of this principle is simply that around the world there is a multiplicity of Ministries of Defence or Departments of Social Service. Thus the name of the parent body is adopted, resulting in the heading **Great Britain. Ministry of Defence,** or **East**

Sussex. Social Services Department.

It is often valuable to have government departments grouped together under the name of the country such as **Great Britain** or **United States**, but where information units acquire large amounts of material from government departments of one country, and no material from other governments it does sometimes appear irritating to have large amounts of material under the same place heading, even though sophisticated subheadings are going to be used. On the other hand, doubt over the specific subheadings for many government departments often means that it is comforting to be able to rely on a broad grouping under the geographical name heading of **Great Britain.**

Managers of information units or cataloguers can obviously modify the general principle to satisfy their own specific user needs, and it must always be remembered that references must be made from various forms of name that have not been used as entry points in the catalogues, leading users across to the forms that have been allowed. Thus under **Social Services** we shall need an entry that reads **Social Services Departments** *see under the geographical name for each local authority.*

Titles

Most titles of works can appear as they stand as either main or added entries. Titles will exist as main entries in the system for items that have no person or corporate body responsible for their intellectual content. Alternatively, titles will be used as main entries for those works which have several people responsible for their intellectual content, and it is impossible to choose a single name. Added entries will also need to be made under any title that can be regarded as a legitimate access point in the catalogue.

References

Throughout this brief overview of general principles about entering works under authors and titles constant mention has been made of a reference structure. However carefully we plan to choose headings that satisfy our users' demands, there will always be cases when users and searchers are unable to work out what form of name has been chosen. Therefore from the very beginning a catalogue must build in a reference structure to allow users to be led from the name they have looked up to the name that has been chosen by the cataloguer. Eventually, the searcher recognizes the broad principles that have been used and learns which form to use.

These broad principles are of course geared to entering works under the name that appears on title pages or other documentary sources. This again presumes that searchers are conversant with other documents produced by those individuals or groups, in order to identify the normal name. For the occasional user, therefore, the reference structure for variant forms of name will always be an essential tool.

OTHER INFORMATION GIVEN IN AN ENTRY

We specifically identified the role of a catalogue as a tool that allows users to choose particular items. This function of choice is important, for there are certain key elements about the physical production of a document or item that are relevant to a subject search. These elements are the edition, along with the name of any editor, etc.; the place of publication; the publisher; the date; a brief statement on length and format; and any special notes that need to be added. Obviously, not all of these elements will be essential for every item in the system but all of them add something to the searcher's ability to choose an item from the retrieval system. Some are more important than others, and the manager of the unit will need to decide which elements to ignore.

The edition statement contains basic information on the up-to-dateness and currency of the document. In many subject areas early editions are totally irrelevant, for they contain old legislation or earlier technical data. Most searchers will require only the most current edition but if the information unit has not been able to acquire that then searchers need to be told that the edition available is not up to date.

The edition statement is therefore important, but for many systems the date is even more important and can take over the function of the edition statement.

The place of publication is often the only indication of the possible geographical bias of a document. Documents published in New York or Delhi will have very different approaches to the subject field, even though they are both written in the English language. Large information units with material from all over the world will need to include the place of publication for all their documents. Small units will be able to ignore places of publication in England but will need to include all places of publication from overseas. As long as searchers understand this system a little time will be saved at the input stage with no major loss in the searching stage.

The name of the publisher is generally included in large systems because it gives valuable information about the quality and standing of the item and will also tell searchers where to get hold of replacement or duplicate copies.

Date of publication is an absolutely fundamental piece of information which ought never to be ignored. Along with an overseas place of publication it gives strong signals about the value and relevance of the item to a particular user's search. An item that is five years old may be totally irrelevant for the searcher's needs.

Interestingly enough, as information becomes more ephemeral the role of the date becomes even more important. If information is produced very speedily, the chances are that it will also date very speedily. A piece of information on legislation or benefit rates that is 18 months old is redundant and should have been weeded out of the system. If it is still in the system for other reasons then the user must be told that the data is now out of date.

The physical description of the item is a very brief statement about length and physical format. This element is to give the searcher an idea about the value of the item to the search. It does not have to be enormously detailed but will need to contain information about the number of pages for a book, eg **400p**, or the format if it is not a book, eg **one video disc**. Extra physical details can also be given if necessary. Thus if a book contains illustrations that might be of value and the element can read **490p. 46 ill**. Similarly, statements about playing speeds, stereo, colour or black-and-white, VHS or Beta formats, film size, etc. need to be given. Finally a statement about the size of the item can finish the physical description. Thus the size of the book in centimetres, or the size of the disc or microfiche is given, eg **23cm**.

These physical description statements can therefore appear fairly complex. However, each piece of information is an important factor in allowing a searcher to choose an item. For all non-print formats that require technical support such as video-players and audio-recording systems, statements about format and size are crucial in allowing the user to decide whether or not it is worth following up the item. For books and other print formats statements about length and size give valuable information about whether the item is detailed enough or wide-ranging enough to satisfy the needs of the user.

There is no denying, however, that the cost of providing this ancillary information may be quite high and many information units will regard these extra details as of limited value. We are back again to the trade-off between input costs and searcher satisfaction. A brief statement about the length of a document, such as **23p.**, is not terribly expensive to provide at the input stage, and may help the searcher greatly when trying to decide between a number of different items. In contrast, the cost of typing up a range of catalogue cards, each giving the number of pages for an item, which then have to be filed under several different access points, may end up being fairly expensive. The extra information when analysed over a period of time may not be that valuable for the searcher.

Different types of user and different materials call for differing amounts of information about the physical characteristics of items. If a full statement of physical description is given, as in the example in figure 6, it can be quite extensive. Therefore, simple punctuation devices are used to break up the various areas of the description, with each block of information separated by a full stop and a dash. Within each of the areas every element of information is introduced by a particular punctuation mark. The role of punctuation is to break up the information into manageable units for visual scanning, and at the same time allow the record to be manipulated inside machine-readable databases. Certain punctuation groups such as the colon and the comma separating place:publisher, date are now so common and accepted that their use is recognized by most users.

361.3'2'0973 — United States. Welfare work —
Manuals
O'Neil, Maria Joan. The general method of
social work practice / Maria Joan O'Neil ;
with a foreword by Carel B. Germain. —
Englewood Cliffs ; London : Prentice-Hall,
c1984. — xiv,351p : ill,forms ; 24cm
Includes index
ISBN 0-13-350554-5 : No price   B85-01552

6 Example of an ISBD from the *British National Bibliography* (taken from the sample page given in figure 9)

Capitalization

The use of capitals in the cataloguing and bibliographic records of items follows normal usage in the written language. Thus we capitalize all nouns, adjectives and verbs in English names, and we always capitalize the first word in a name. This follows normal written practice.

Catalogues have always followed normal English usage in their capitalization of titles of works. This means that the first word of a title, proper nouns and proper adjectives are capitalized but other words are not, eg **Community information services**. The slight difficulty here is that when most people write the title of a work as part of a piece of text, every word in the title is capitalized. This is to separate out the title of a work from the rest of the text around it. Similarly, many publishers will capitalize all the words in a title when it is listed in a bibliography or reading list. This then causes confusion in an information unit when staff are suddenly instructed to stop capitalizing all parts of a title when they enter it into a catalogue.

The arguments in favour of not capitalizing all the words in a title in a catalogue entry are mainly to do with common sense and the effort of typing every word in a title with a capital letter. Also, if every word in the title has its first letter capitalized, then the large amount of information that is being carried by the whole of the catalogue entry is made confusing by the surfeit of capital letters.

International Standard Bibliographic Description

The basic rules and principles for producing headings and physical descriptions of items have been evolved and agreed upon by librarians throughout the world over many decades. This slow process of agreement was speeded up by the introduction of large machine-readable databases whereby information about books and documents could be disseminated around the world through on-line systems and the merging of computer files. From this process there has emerged an International Standard Bibliographic Description (ISBD) for each major format of material (see figure 6).

These ISBDs are designed to allow libraries to have the fullest amount of information necessary on all bibliographic databases, which can then be modified to allow each library to have that part of the description that it requires for its own particular user needs. There is thus a sound argument for information units that use only a small part of the bibliographic description to do so in a format which accords with the general conventions of the international standard. This reduces the potential for confusion and allows users, searchers and information staff to move towards an agreed and recognizable structure for their information dissemination and handling.

Many small systems, such as school libraries, still reject the international standard and, for example, capitalize the first letter of every word in a title. They do this on the grounds that it matches the teaching of English in their curriculum. There are many other units that do not follow any particular standard, and have their information in a very different order from that which is suggested by the general principles. However, there are few reasons for rejecting an internationally agreed standard that is used in a majority of libraries and information units and which users and searchers are slowly coming to recognize because of their exposure to it in a variety of different situations. User education, staff training and communication between information units all tend to suggest that following such a standard is sensible.

The standard, of course, relates to the order of information in the entry, and always allows information units to vary the quantity of that information. If an information unit requires merely title, author, date and classmark then it is quite at liberty to provide only that. The standard suggests though, that this minimal information should be presented in the format of **title/author. – date.classmark.**

CATALOGUING CODES

The production of author-title catalogues involves a series of decisions about who or what is the author; what is the title; what additional access points are needed; and what references will be needed to link it all together; finally how can the bibliographic and descriptive information be laid out for maximum effect. There are also stylistic conventions such as punctuation, capitalization and layout which will need to be decided on and adhered to. Many small information units resolve these problems in an ad hoc way as they grow, in a fashion that suits their particular users.

As we have seen, however, there is an International Standard Bibliographic Description for most visible forms of material. There are also international conventions over forms of heading and added entries that are followed in a wide variety of information units around the world. It is in order to document such international conventions that cataloguing codes are produced and accepted by the libraries and information units that use them.

Small information units that are making such decisions as they grow have two options open to them. Firstly, they can evolve their own ad hoc rules and stick to them, making decisions as problems arise and attempting to ensure consistency. Secondly they can adopt an internationally agreed set of cataloguing rules which cover a series of problems which are far greater than they will ever meet but ensure a level of consistency for the future.

If an information unit adopts the first course then for a reasonable period of time the unit's catalogue will also act as a record, or 'authority file' for the decisions that have been made. Thus an indexer can merely consult the file to see how a similar problem was tackled last time and follow the same principle. However, as catalogues and files get larger and larger it becomes more and more difficult to follow this course of action, and the series of decisions will need to be documented and set down as a working authority file.

Published cataloguing codes

There are several published codes and rules, of which the most famous and all-embracing is the *Anglo-American Cataloguing Rules*, second edition published in 1978 by the American Library Association and the Library Association. This set of rules aims to cover all the problems involved in author-title cataloguing and information work, covering the majority of physical formats of material within libraries. The main emphasis is naturally on traditional book formats and there is a tendency to try to squeeze all variant physical forms into a structure that suits traditional books. Nonetheless, it is an essential tool in producing author-title catalogues and indexes, and its role is widened by the fact that a concise version exists, known as the *Concise AACR2*, published in 1981 and available from the Library Association. This code is short, very manageable, and designed specifically for the smaller or less complex library that requires simplicity and conciseness rather than the detail required for the wide range of bibliographic material that exists in the fully developed academic libraries that the full code is designed for.

Two other codes of cataloguing rules are relevant in areas of non-book format. The Canadian Library Association's *Non-book materials: the organisation of integrated collections* offers detailed support for catalogues and indexes that cover specifically non-text and non-book materials. There is also a code of cataloguing produced by the National Council for Educational Technology and the Library Association entitled *Non-book materials cataloguing rules*. These two texts give help and assistance in an area of catalogue production that can cause the greatest amount of difficulty.

Although the large majority of small information units are far more concerned with the subject approach to information than the more traditional author-title access, and therefore might regard the latter as too unimportant to merit much planning and systemization, there will always tend to be some form of author-title approach, however limited. All information units grow, and even a limited author-title catalogue or index will eventually need some sort of consistency and internal logic. It is therefore an excellent idea to start off using a tool such as the *Concise AACR2* which gives a basis for growth and consistency over the years.

FILING

There is always the clerical but essential task of filing and of deciding how to file alphabetically. Rather like the decisions concerning forms of authors' names and choice of heading in the author-title catalogue, the rules for filing are relatively simple yet have an enormous effect on the resulting sequence if a consistent set of decisions is followed. The British Standards Institution and the American Library Association have both produced sets of filing rules, with the American Library Association's Rules for filing catalogue cards being a basic standard in a number of library systems.

Word-by-word or letter-by-letter

The first key decision is whether or not the arrangement will ignore gaps between words and file 'letter-by-letter', or whether each similar word will be grouped followed by a space and then the next word in the string, giving a 'word-by-word' arrangement. This is best shown by an example:

Word-by-word	*Letter-by-letter*
New Amsterdam	New Amsterdam
New England	Newark
New wives for old	New England

New York	Newman
Newark	Newt
Newman	New wives for old
Newt	New York

As can be seen, the simple difference between letter-by-letter filing and word-by-word filing results in a very different sequence, and it really is important that people filing into the system and people searching the system have some idea of how the arrangement is structured. In very general terms letter-by-letter filing is probably easier for the person doing the filing, whilst word-by-word filing is probably easier for the searching process. Individuals tend to have a natural inclination to file using one method or the other and it is therefore important that when any filing that takes place simple decisions are made over which system is to be adopted. It can be seen that if the two systems of filing are muddled up and both take place within the file, chaos will result, with **New York** appearing in two separate places. If the file contains authors' names, titles and subjects that contain the heading 'New York' then it can be seen that the whole system will become unusable if such mistakes are built in.

When there are a number of different types of entry appearing at the same heading, for example **London**, then a decision obviously needs to be made about how to subarrange. For example:

London
London Baptist Association
London – History
London, Jack
London life in the eighteenth century
London – Museums
London School of Economics
London, Vera

These entries have all been arranged strictly alphabetically according to the words in the headings, disregarding all the punctuation. This results in a simple filing system, but can cause the user some dissatisfaction because there might be a tendency to assume that **London, Jack** and **London, Vera** will file next to each other and **London Baptist Association** and **London School of Economics** should also file next to each other. Thus some filing systems group together all the names of people starting with the same surname and then follow it with the other headings starting with the same word. This gives users an understandable sequence, but causes confusion to the filers unless they are told exactly what is happening. Of course, in a printed list or catalogue these subtleties of arrangement are clear because the whole page can be seen, but in a card catalogue only one entry at a time can be seen and the structure of the whole file is never obvious. It is for such card catalogues that filing rules become so important.

There is also a wide range of small clerical decisions about particular problems involving filing. These problems can be identified in the American Library Association's *Rules for filing catalogue cards* or the British Standards Institution's rules and cover difficulties such as initials – **AA** or **BBC** normally file before words or acronyms such as **Unesco** which are filed as if they were a straightforward word. Abbreviations such as **Mr** or **St** are normally filed as if they were spelt out in full. In many systems, numerals are filed as if they were spelt out although a growing number of indexes and catalogues file numerals at the very beginning of the sequence before **A**.

Compound names such as **Hall Brown** file in the sequence as if they were single words, and hyphens are ignored so that **Hall Brown** without a hyphen will file in the same place as **Hall-Brown** with a hyphen. The only exception is if the hyphenated prefix is an incomplete word such as **pre-** or **co-**.

Filing rules, like cataloguing rules, try to ensure a level of consistency and common sense that will allow the searcher and the indexer to match decisions as far as possible. In both cases consistency is the essential factor, even if occasionally the decision might be the wrong one. The great problem with inconsistency or even changes of policy is that multiple sequences can build up and searchers obtain only a small proportion of the relevant available material because the remainder is entered under a subject heading which has been misfiled elsewhere in the sequence.

ABSTRACTING
In many information-retrieval systems the information given about each item after the heading is the basic cataloguing description containing the bibliographic information that will allow the item to be located within the information unit or acquired from elsewhere.

However, for many information-retrieval systems these minimal bibliographic or descriptive cataloguing data are insufficient to allow searchers to decide the relevance of an item. It is the role of an abstract to offer a resumé of the contents of an item, so that the searcher can assess its relevance without having to consult the original. It is therefore to be seen as a sifting device, a part of the retrieval system that will remove the irrelevant and allow the searcher to concentrate on the essential.

Abstracting can be done in an information unit for particular types of material, for particular user groups or possibly for particular subject areas that are not covered by any of the expensive printed abstracting services. Few information units consider abstracting more than a small proportion of their total input, and most would tend to select items for abstracting that were novel, particularly relevant, inaccessible through any service or vital to a particular user group. Such items selected for abstracting would tend to be disseminated as part of a regular weekly or monthly abstracting bulletin produced by the information unit. The regular dissemination of abstracts through such a bulletin yields eventually an in-house database which can be kept manually either as part of the normal catalogue or separately. Alternatively it can be put onto a microcomputer for future computerized searching as the database gets larger and larger.

The actual task of producing abstracts for items is expensive in staff time, and it requires a fair degree of skill to be able to read an item and turn it into a valuable 100-word abstract. Nonetheless, the needs of certain users and the requirements of certain physical forms of material result in abstracting skills being an essential part of the work pattern of many information units.

Traditionally abstracts have fallen into particular groups. Informative abstracts are those that actually attempt, in certain circumstances, to replace the document. They range in length from 100 to possibly 500 words and concentrate on the quantitative or qualitative information contained in the document.

Indicative abstracts merely give some resumé of what a paper or piece of information is trying to say. They are normally short, and rarely attempt to replace the original document. They act merely as an alerting and selection tool. They are obviously easier and rather quicker to produce and may involve less subject expertise on the part of the abstracter.

There are other sorts of abstracts, particularly critical abstracts, slanted abstracts and abbreviated abstracts but they all are attempting to summarize and précis the original. The various types of abstract are not as clear-cut as this summary suggests, with the personal style of the abstracter having a greater effect on the end product than any attempt to follow a rigorous policy of producing indicative or informative abstracts. The task of turning a 6,000-word article into a 100-word abstract can involve problems over what an article is trying to say. Many journals now require an author to produce his own abstract at the beginning of the article.

Abstracting techniques

There are quite a large number of sets of instructions for abstracters produced by the various published abstracting services, but a valuable standard in this area is the American National Standards Institution's *Standard for writing abstracts* which covers many of the key processes for writing abstracts and gives a number of examples of the different sorts of abstracts that can be produced from the same article (see figure 7).

The title, resumé of contents, introduction, conclusions and any final recommendations are the key of parts of any text to be studied when abstracting. Any introduction to the text is obviously important, but the whole item must be scanned through and final conclusions absorbed before any attempt is made to produce the abstract. During this rapid scan brief notes are taken giving the major points to be covered in the abstract. From these brief notes the final abstract can be produced, reducing all redundant and repetitive terminology to a minimum to keep it within the minimum length.

Although there are a number of useful introductory guides in this area, with Maizell's *Abstracting scientific and technical literature* and Borko and Bernier's *Abstracting concepts and methods* being good examples, little can substitute for detailed experience. Initial attempts will normally produce abstracts that are too long but after a time the experienced abstracter becomes confident that the detailed scan of the original item can result in a 100-word resumé that contains all the factors of importance in the text. Figure 8 gives examples of abstracts of different types of material.

The growth in on-line bibliographic databases has meant that the abstract has become a very essential part of information-retrieval systems. As we shall see in other sections the majority of such databases use natural-language indexing systems – that is the index

Examples of abstracts

AN INFORMATIVE ABSTRACT
Traditional cooling systems in the third world.

Ecologist, 6 (2), Feb. 1976, 60–64.

As demonstrated by the Maziara cooling jar, indigenous technologies are generally more suited to the developing world than advanced Western technologies. Early in the morning the cooling jar is filled and during the day water seeps through the porous, unglazed ceramic jar, maintaining a wet outside surface. Some water from the outside evaporates, keeping the drinking water in the jar cool. In tests in Egypt, with outside temperatures ranging from 19 to 36 degC, the water remained constantly at 20 degC. The remainder of the water may be collected as it drips down the outside of the jar, and drunk; tests showed this water to be pure enough for drinking even when the water inside the jar was contaminated. The cooling jar compared very favourably in energy consumption terms with a mechanical air conditioning unit. Porous water jugs, and dampened reed matting used in conjunction with wind-catching towers, tall narrow courtyards, wind shafts leading to basement water cisterns and water jars mounted in window openings may be used to cool rooms. Perishable foods may be stored and cooled by placing them in a glazed inner jar inside a porous water jar.

AN INDICATIVE ABSTRACT
Traditional cooling systems in the third world.

Ecologist, 6 (2), Feb. 1976, 60–64.

The merits of indigenous, as opposed to Western technologies, are illustrated in discussing the Maziara cooling jar. The mechanism of the jar is described. Test results, showing that water remained cool in the jar all day, despite widely varying ambient temperatures, and that water seeping through the jar was purer than water contained in it, are reported. Cooling jars compare favourably with mechanical air-conditioning units, in energy consumption terms. Other room or food cooling systems prevalent in developing countries based on damp reed matting, cool cellars and courtyards and water-cooling jars are described with illustrations.

A SHORT ABSTRACT
Traditional cooling systems in the third world.

Ecologist, 6 (2), Feb. 1976, 60–64.

Maziara cooling jars, and other devices based on evaporative cooling and induced air flow, are used to illustrate the merits of indigenous technologies in the developing world.

7 **Examples of different kinds of abstract from the ANSI *Standard for writing abstracts***

AN ABSTRACT OF A REVIEW ARTICLE
Recent advances in the ring oven technique – a review.
H. Weisz.

Analyst, 101 (1200), Mar. 1976, 152–160.

This technique is a form of spot analysis carried out on filter paper, in which substances to be identified or determined are concentrated in sharply developed, well defined, circular lines by the heat barrier action of the edge of the control bore hole of the ring oven's heating block. Separation can be carried out on a single drop. The application of the ring oven in the 1) qualitative analysis of metal ions; 2) determination of cations and anions; 3) analysis of organic substances (herbicides, vitamins); 4) radiochemical analysis; and, 5) air pollution studies, is reviewed. Its use in combination with other analytical techniques, and new applications involving adsorption rather than a heat barrier, using catalysed reactions, and for testing unstable reaction products are described. Applications since 1961 are emphasised. (104 refs.)

AN ABSTRACT OF A MONOGRAPH
Operations research.
J. Singh.
Harmondsworth: Penguin Books, 1971 (Pelican Library of Business and Management).

Attempts to give the manager an understanding of the mathematical techniques underlying operations research, which, the author maintains, is a blend of mathematical theory and practical insight. Introductory chapters on statistical summarisation, specification and inference are followed by chapters on network analysis, linear programming, game theory, queuing theory and Monte Carlo simulation.

AN ABSTRACT OF A NEWSPAPER ARTICLE
£300,000 centre for problem children is given go-ahead.
Birmingham Post, 1 July 1976, p. 3.

Despite local protests, government approval has been given for an assessment centre for sixteen problem children in local authority care. The centre will be built in the Danescourt residential area in Tettenhall, Wolverhampton.

8 Examples of abstracts from different types of material from the ANSI *Standard for writing abstracts* terms used for searching are derived from the abstracts themselves rather than an indexer assigning particular index terms to each item. Thus, for the majority of databases, the 100 words in the abstract are reduced by the exclusion of all the redundant literary devices such as 'and', 'but' or 'if' and the remaining concept terms are used as access points in an inverted post-coordinate file. These terms are then searched using a strategy known as Boolean search logic. This allows the various terms to be joined together and search statements to be built up. Software that allows internally-produced abstracts to be turned into an inverted database file already exists for micro-computers, as is discussed in Chapter 6 on computer applications. This means that abstracts produced now can eventually form part of a natural-language database as the information unit grows and develops.

PHYSICAL FORMS OF CATALOGUES

The physical form of a catalogue, like the physical arrangement of items in an information unit, has an enormous effect on its use and value. Catalogues and indexes tend not to be tools that are used by the end-user, often appearing complex and cumbersome and offer-ing a rather poor satisfaction rate for the amount of time spent on searching. The rapid growth of computerized catalogues, using either microcomputers or terminals networked to a larger system as discussed in the section on computer applications (Chapter 6), has in many ways transformed this, with many end-users quite happily consulting traditional library catalogues through terminals because of their speed and convenience. However, the more traditional physical forms of card and printed list catalogues, along with the slightly more recent microfiche, still tend to be seen as tools for the information officer or librarian to use and consult, with the end-user being given the final fruits of the labour. This is often because the size and complexity of library catalogues and indexes put up a bar-rier between the user and the information store.

Card catalogues are the primary physical form of most manual indexes and catalogues. Cards measuring five inches by three or six inches by four are cheap to buy, they can be typed on and the process of inserting new cards in the sequence is simple. Cheap duplicating systems can be used to produce multiple copies of catalogue cards for added entries under different classmarks, or under different author and title access points. Metal or wooden catalogue card drawers can be bought gradually in pairs or small groups and linked together so that a system can grow quite cheaply.

One of the major costs of card catalogues is of course the filing process itself, which is quite slow and therefore expensive in terms of staff time. One of the great advantages of the growth of computerized indexes and catalogues is that this filing process is removed. However, many small information units have access to relatively cheap staff time through volunteers or assistants who can help in the filing process, as long as the rigorous rules about filing discussed above are carefully explained and laid down for all the filers.

Sheaf catalogues are small, looseleaf folders with the cataloguing or indexing information typed onto paper slips or sheafs. An advantage of such a system is that multiple copies of each clip can be typed using ordinary carbon paper, whilst the disadvantage is that filing is quite difficult because of the metal rings that have to be opened to insert the slips in the right place in the binder. The book-type format of the binder does allow the catalogue index to be skimmed through quite quickly and the various binders can be consulted by different people at the same time in the information unit rather more easily than a card catalogue.

Book-form catalogues have become almost entirely redundant because of the cost of printing and production, being retained only by the large national libraries. This has been transformed for the small information unit with the advent of word-processing and database-management packages which allow the catalogue file to be held on a floppy disc, updated as necessary and printed out on computer stationery at regular intervals.

The huge advantage of a book-form catalogue is that a large number of entries can be scanned very quickly whilst retaining some sort of browsing process. Thus five or six pages of computer stationery can include a large number of entries and the searcher can see the relationship of various items to each other and make decisions about the relevance of particular texts. It is probably true that computer-produced catalogues are merely a by-product of the main catalogue being held on a microcomputer, and the growing cost of computer stationery means that many information units will baulk at the prospect of printing frequently multiple copies of their indexes and catalogues. The book catalogue does, however, have very high user satisfaction, and can also be disseminated to other institutions. Users might be prepared to pay sufficient to cover the production costs.

Microform catalogues came into being as a method of allowing the enormous catalogues of academic and public libraries to be stored in a reasonable amount of space. They obviously involve some form of computer production and are really relevant only for extremely large catalogues and indexes that need to be produced in multiple copies at frequent intervals. They can be irritating because they involve microfiche readers but the end product is of course the same sort of browsing ability that traditional book-form catalogues had.

Computer-held catalogues are a recent phenomenon. Originally most computer catalogues were primarily produced in order to print out either book-form catalogues or miroform catalogues. Rapidly changing technology has meant that on-line public-access catalogues, with users using a terminal to link into a large database, are now becoming normal in many academic and public libraries. When linked to a computerized issue system and computerized membership and reservation system they offer powerful tools for allowing users to identify what they want, and then reserve them.

At the other end of the spectrum the growth of cheap microcomputers with database-management software has meant that a small information unit can now input its cataloguing information onto a floppy disc and allow users to search a continuously updated file. School libraries and learning-resource centres have been experimenting with such systems for some time now, and a number of small information units have computerized indexes using micros such as the IBM PC, Apricot or BBC. This is discussed more fully in the section on computer applications in Chapter 6.

The Centre for Cataloguing Research at the Library of the University of Bath has produced a large amount of information on both the physical format of catalogues and the information contained within catalogues and its relationship to user satisfaction. The importance of simplicity, ease of use and the advantages of relatively cheap and 'dirty' systems that actually work are the main findings from much of this research work.

3   An introduction to the subject approach

THE SUBJECT APPROACH

Information-retrieval systems are primarily concerned with the subject approach. Although we have discussed access to the system through authors and titles the majority of users are interested in the subject approach to information.

Because the users and searchers of information-retrieval systems communicate through language the whole emphasis in the subject approach is on how to match the words that clients make use of with the words that the authors of the relevant texts have used. Because of the problems inherent in the meanings of words, and the relationships that exist between concepts and the words that describe them, most retrieval systems use a specialized vocabulary or retrieval language. This retrieval language can be a real language, using the sorts of words that searchers use, or it can be an artificial language such as a classification scheme so that the problems to do with meanings of words are reduced and the importance of identifying and showing relationships is enhanced.

The various sections that follow discuss different sorts of retrieval languages or vocabularies, as well as identifying some of the systems that allow the words in the vocabularies to be joined together to form strings that accurately describe the subject content of items. The primary function of an indexing vocabulary is to ensure consistency and facilitate this matching process between the searcher and the information in the store.

Specificity

An important element in the index language is how specific it is to be. Does the vocabulary or classification scheme allow specific concepts such as **rate arrears,** or does the vocabulary keep all such items under a general classmark or subject heading for **rates?** Does **elec-**

tricity supply debt go at that specific access point or is it kept at one of the general concepts **debt** or **electricity**? Such decisions have to be made when the indexing vocabulary is designed or adopted. It is this specificity in the indexing vocabulary which affects the precision the user receives. Precision, as we have shown, is the ability of the retrieval system to provide the most relevant items and reject any non-relevant or less relevant items. If the user requires **electricity supply debts** then the provision of that term in the vocabulary allows him to access the system at that specific point. There the user will receive those items that discuss electricity supply debt and nothing else. If the vocabulary is not specific, and the user has to search under **debt** or **electricity supply**, then during that search a large number of irrelevant items related to debt in general or other types of debt or the electricity industry in general will be retrieved. Thus the specificity of the vocabulary affects the level of precision that the user can achieve in the system. As we saw in Chapter 1 on users, precision is effectively a measure of users' effort. If precision is very bad the user has to spend considerable time searching through irrelevant material in order to identify the items that are of particular use.

In general terms, the larger the vocabulary the more specific the terminology in it. Most vocabularies contain all the generalized terms for the subject field, and therefore as the vocabulary size increases it is the more specific terms that are becoming part of the indexing language. Thus a vocabulary with a large number of access points and a system that allows those access points to be synthesized is more specific than an indexing vocabulary that has only a few terms and which does not allow synthesis. It is these factors that will be taken into account when an information unit either adopts a particular indexing vocabulary or decides to produce its own.

The corollary of the specificity–precision relationship is that if a vocabulary is less specific, and the user is forced to search through a large number of possibly irrelevant items the users' recall is increased because in that searching process the chances are that an increased number of moderately relevant items will be retrieved. Thus if the user searches through the debt sequence in the retrieval file material will be found that is relevant to the problem of electricity supply debt but which is not necessarily part of the problem and would not have been indexed under that term if the vocabulary had been highly specific.

Thus, non-specific vocabularies give the users a higher level of recall, but at the same time do not allow the retrieval of only those items which give high precision for that particular search. Highly specific vocabularies, on the other hand, ensure the retrieval of all highly relevant items, but will miss all the related items.

The subject indexing process

The subject indexing process involves two distinct elements although in practice an individual indexer tends to blur them together. Firstly an item needs to be read and understood so that the indexer can analyse the concepts that exist within the item. There are obviously some difficulties involved in this process, to do with the subject knowledge of the indexer and the social and educational constraints within which the indexer is working. The indexers' knowledge of the user and the use to which the information will be put also have a bearing on this process of analysing concepts. The indexer will then attempt to translate these concepts into the language of the retrieval system. As we shall see, this might be a classification scheme, an alphabetical list of subject headings or a thesaurus. The importance of this translation process is that it allows the indexer to turn an analysis of the concepts contained in the item into the language which the searcher will be using. As the function of the retrieval system is to ensure that this matching process takes place, efficient translation into this vocabulary is important.

Vocabularies vary in terms of their specificity, but all retrieval systems work on the assumption that an indexer will use the most specific terms possible for each item. If this does not happen, problems occur. If the searcher cannot be confident that the indexer has used the most specific terms available in the vocabulary, designing search strategies becomes difficult. For example, if users require information about housing benefit they will tend to look under the heading **Housing benefit**. If only some information exists at that subject heading whilst other equally relevant information exists at the broader term **Benefits** then satisfaction rates will be extremely low.

Exhaustivity

The indexer must also decide how many of the concepts which each item is about are actually going to be indexed. Assuming that the indexer will use the vocabulary as specifically as possible, there are likely to be large numbers of differing themes and concepts in any one item which could be indexed. There will be certain major themes and topics and a wider range of subsidiary themes and topics.

For example, the conceptual analysis of a document might indicate that there are six themes contained in it. Themes A and B appear to be major and C, D, E and F appear rather minor. If indexing is to be totally exhaustive then all six themes will need to be indexed. However, four of the themes are less important. When a searcher retrieves this particular item in response to a search strategy formulated for one of the minor themes, the relevance of this particular item will not be very high. However, if we do not index the four subsidiary themes then a user who requires all of the items on that theme – even if they are not completely relevant – will be unsatisfied.

Thus the exhaustivity of the indexing process relates directly to the amount of recall that the particular retrieval system provides. If indexing is very exhaustive then a user will retrieve many items at each access point in the system, some of which will be rather less relevant because that particular index term was a minor theme in the document. Of course, the corollary is also true that if we index only the two important themes in an item – A and B in our example – and ignore the rest, then the searcher will retrieve only the highly relevant items under each access point. All the other items that discuss this theme in a less relevant way will not be retrieved.

Recall, the ability of a retrieval system to retrieve all relevant items on a topic, and precision, the ability of a retrieval system to cut out or reject the irrelevant items on a topic, are thus closely related to the exhaustivity of the indexing process, as well as the specificity of the terms in the vocabulary.

CLASSIFICATION SCHEMES AND THE SUBJECT APPROACH

Classification schemes have a long history in the retrieval of subject information because they seem to offer an approach that is inherently neat and valuable to the user. As we saw in Chapter 1 on the physical arrangement of materials, a classification scheme tries to indicate the relationships between subjects by grouping them into a particular order. This grouping process allows users to see the strength of relationships between particular concepts and should allow the user to identify a 'map' of all the various relationships within a particular broad subject area.

This idea of a conceptual map of a subject has a number of interesting advantages. It obviously reduces the need to know exactly what a specific subject is actually called, for, if the user can identify the various relationships that each subject has, it should be possible to find the required subject area by browsing through either a physical arrangement of material or through some catalogue, index or database. Classification schemes have always been seen as having a particular role of stimulating information searching, by showing the searcher links and relationships which might not have been identified at the initial search stage. This role of showing links and relationships and identifying possible gaps in the subject field has meant that classification as an approach has always been an integral part of the research process.

From very early times a process of classification has been evident in much philosophy and science. Based on the research into classifying animals or chemical elements, a body of theory about producing classification schemes has emerged. As libraries and information-retrieval systems became involved in retrieving information in fairly sophisticated ways it was obvious that some of this thinking on the production of classification schemes would be absorbed into the profession. It is probably not true to say that the traditional bibliographic classification schemes that will be discussed in the next chapter are based primarily on a particular theory or body of classification knowledge, but it is clear that in all the successful parts of the traditional bibliographic classification schemes used in many libraries we can identify particular theories at work.

One particular aspect of classification schemes is that they are an extremely useful way of actually arranging material. This is because each classification scheme uses a notation to show its particular arrangement and grouping of concepts and therefore this notation acts as a very efficient shorthand for some fairly complex concepts. It is obviously far easier to use this shorthand notation for arranging documents and other materials than it would be to use the alphabetical words that describe the subjects. Thus, although many retrieval systems reject classification schemes as being rather cumbersome and dated they may still retain one for the final arrangement of materials on shelves or in filing cabinets.

Classification schemes obviously require a large amount of effort to the design stage, when the decisions are being made about the types of grouping and the links and relationships that are going to be identified by the particular classification scheme.

Once the scheme has been produced a particular information unit may decide to adopt it because it covers the subject discipline of the unit and matches the sorts of needs that users of the unit have expressed. Thus an information unit might adopt one of the traditional or bibliographic classification schemes because the unit contains a wide range of differing subject fields and, perhaps, a group of users that are similar to users of public libraries. However, another unit might have a very specialist subject requirement and can identify a particular scheme produced by a similar information unit that will cover the subject area precisely.

Alternatively, an information unit might decide that no scheme exists that is particularly relevant and that it will be worthwhile producing a classification scheme of its own. Although this latter course might be expensive and time-consuming many information units decide that it is preferable to have a custom-made scheme than make do with second best.

A classified retrieval language or classification scheme has a number of different component parts. The main part is the schedules which are lists of concepts arranged in the particular order that the classification scheme is trying to show. This order will be decided upon by the makers of the scheme and will try to indicate links and relationships between subjects. It will also show the strength of the relationships between concepts by the extent to which it separates those concepts in the schedules. Onto this schedule is put a notation, which is simply a code or artificial language which keeps items in the desired order once they have been classified. It is important not to confuse the notation with the classification scheme itself. The notation is merely an artificial constraint which keeps items in a particular order; it is the schedules of the classification scheme which determine the order itself. Finally the scheme itself is provided with an index.

Classification schemes can be used in two ways in retrieval systems. As already mentioned they are important ways of actually arranging items on shelves or in filing cabinets. By doing so they stimulate browsing and ensure that the user is shown relationships and maybe led to other linked concepts that may be relevant. The classification scheme can also be used to arrange catalogues, indexes and databases. Such a classified catalogue can be seen in the *British National Bibliography* (see figure 9), in which is an excellent example of an arrangement using the Dewey decimal classification scheme, discussed in more detail in Chapter 4. Such a classified catalogue can duplicate the arrangement of materials on shelves or in filing cabinets, in which case it is there primarily to allow users to search a large physical arrangement of stock in a more efficient manner in the catalogue. Alternatively, a classified catalogue may support a different physical arrangement such as one by report number, author or some other non-subject approach.

The whole essence of a classified arrangement is the relationships that can be shown and the increased relevance and value gained by the user from each individual search. If this is to be the case then obviously decisions made by the classification scheme maker on the particular groupings and relationships shown are very important.

Classification schemes available today have been produced by one of two different approaches. The first approach, enumerative, is a result of the traditional ideas and theories that emerged from the makers of the scientific and philosophical classification schemes reaching right back to the Greeks. This enumerative theory is in some part behind the majority of the large traditional bibliographic classification schemes that can be seen in most academic and public libraries.

An alternative model for producing a classification scheme is to use an 'analytico-synthetic' or 'faceted' approach in the construction of schedules. This approach emerged during this century and is the methodology that is used to produce the classification schemes that are being constructed today. Although the notations which result from classification schemes using either of these methodologies may not look different from each other, the process of making the actual classification scheme and, more importantly, the process for assigning each classmark by the classifier in the information unit is quite different. Because both enumerative and faceted classification schemes are available for information units to adopt, a basic understanding of the difference between these two methodologies is important.

Enumerative classification schemes
Enumerative classification schemes are produced by a steady process of division, resulting in very specific detailed concepts being

THE BRITISH NATIONAL BIBLIOGRAPHY   183

361.1'0941 — Great Britain. Social problems —
Topics for discussion groups — For schools
Mullen, Peter. Questions for society 2 : in
pictures / written by Peter Mullen ; drawn by
Martin Pitts. — London : Edward Arnold,
1984. — 64p : ill ; 25cm
ISBN 0-7131-7323-8 (pbk) : No price : CIP
rev.   B84-31026

361.1'0941 — Great Britain. Urban regions. Social
problems. Geographical aspects
Royal Scottish Geographical Society. *Symposium*
(3rd). Quality of life and human welfare :
proceedings of the Third Royal Scottish
Geographical Society Symposium / edited by
M. Pacione and G. Gordon. — Norwich : Geo,
c1984. — vii,120p : ill,maps ; 22cm
Includes bibliographies
ISBN 0-86094-142-6 : No price   B85-01242

361.1'09417 — Ireland (Republic). Social problems
[New deal (Dublin)]. New deal : incorporating
FLAC file. — Nov.-Dec. '81. — Dublin (3
North Earl St., Dublin 1) : Free Legal Advice
Centres, 1981. —   v. : ill,ports ; 30cm
Six issues yearly. — Continues: FLAC file
ISSN 0332-3676 = New deal (Dublin) : No
price   B85-03216

361.3 — SOCIAL WORK

361.3 — Welfare work
Creative change : a cognitive-humanistic
approach to social work practice / Howard
Goldstein, editor with Harvey C. Hilbert and
Judith C. Hilbert. — New York ; London :
Tavistock, 1984. — xiv,306p : ill ; 23cm. —
(Social science paperbacks ; 282)
Includes bibliographies and index
ISBN 0-422-78650-0 (pbk) : No price : CIP
rev.   B84-33811

Women, the family, and social work / edited by
Eve Brook and Ann Davis. — London :
Tavistock, 1985. — 1v. — (Tavistock library
of social work practice)
Includes bibliographies and index
ISBN 0-422-77940-7 (cased) : £10.95 : CIP
entry (June)
ISBN 0-422-77950-4 (pbk) : £5.50   B85-13457

361.3'023'41 — Great Britain. Welfare work —
Career guides
Davies, Maureen. Working in community care /
[written and researched by Maureen Davies].
— Sheffield : COIC, c1983. — 15p : ill,ports ;
30cm. — (Working in ; no.71)
ISBN 0-86110-293-2 (unbound) : No price
                                                  B85-07222

361.3'068'4 — Social services. Policies. Decision
making
Tropman, John E. Policy management in the
human services / John E. Tropman. — New
York : Columbia University Press,
1984. — xvii,296p : ill ; 24cm
Bibliography: p277-284. — Includes index
ISBN 0-231-05616-1 (cased) : £30.35
ISBN 0-231-05615-x (pbk) : No price   B85-07941

361.3'07'1173 — United States. Welfare workers.
Professional education
Baskind, Frank R. Defining generalist social
work practice / Frank R. Baskind. — Lanham,
Md. : University Press of America,
c1984. — xiv,127p : ill ; 22cm
Bibliography: p109-114
ISBN 0-8191-3718-9 (cased) : No price
ISBN 0-8191-3719-7 (pbk) : £8.50   B85-06847

361.3'0941 — Great Britain. Welfare work
Issues in social welfare / edited by Howard
Jones. — Cardiff : University College, 1984. —
i,153p ; 21cm
Cover title
No price (pbk)   B85-06615

Theory and practice in social work / edited by
Roy Bailey and Phil Lee. — Oxford :
Blackwell, 1982. — viii,238p : ill ; 23cm
Includes bibliographies and index
ISBN 0-631-12653-8 (cased) : No price : CIP
rev.
ISBN 0-631-12709-7 (pbk) : No price   B82-04584

361.3'2 — Welfare work. Casework. Task-centred
treatment
Goldberg, E. Mathilde. Problems, tasks and
outcomes : the evaluation of task centred
casework in three settings / E. Matilda [i.e.
Mathilde] Goldberg, Jane Gibbons, Ian
Sinclair. — London : Allen & Unwin, 1985. —
viii,274p ; 22cm. — (National Institute social
services library ; no.47)
Includes bibliographies and index
ISBN 0-04-361053-6 : £20.00 : CIP rev.
                                                  B84-28356

361.3'2'019 — Great Britain. Welfare workers.
Stress
Fineman, Stephen. Social work stress and
intervention / Stephen Fineman. — Aldershot :
Gower, 1984. — 214p ; 21cm
Bibliography: p167-172. — Includes index
ISBN 0-566-00664-2 : £14.50 : CIP entry
(Mar.)   B85-01511

361.3'2'0973 — United States. Welfare work —
Manuals
O'Neil, Maria Joan. The general method of
social work practice / Maria Joan O'Neil ;
with a foreword by Carel B. Germain. —
Englewood Cliffs ; London : Prentice-Hall,
c1984. — xiv,351p : ill,forms ; 24cm
Includes index
ISBN 0-13-350554-5 : No price   B85-01552

361.3'23 — Counselling. Responsibility
Nelson-Jones, Richard. Personal responsibility
counselling and therapy : an integrative
approach / Richard Nelson-Jones. — London :
Harper & Row, 1984. — 214p ; 21cm
Bibliography: p196-205. — Includes index
ISBN 0-06-318299-8 (pbk) : No price : CIP
rev.   B84-20555

361.6 — PUBLIC SOCIAL WELFARE

361.6 — Social development. Economic aspects
The Economics of human betterment :
proceedings of Section F (Economics) of the
British Association for the Advancement of
Science, Sussex 1983 / edited by Kenneth E.
Boulding. — London : Macmillan, 1984. —
xiii,220p : ill ; 23cm
Includes bibliographies and index
ISBN 0-333-36375-2 (cased) : £25.00 : CIP rev.
ISBN 0-333-36376-0 (pbk) : No price
                                        B84-14380

361.6'0941 — Great Britain. Public welfare services
Graham, Hilary. Health and welfare / Hilary
Graham. — London : Macmillan, 1985. —
[148]p : ill ; 22cm. — (Issues in sociology)
Includes bibliography and index
ISBN 0-333-37191-7 (pbk) : £2.45 : CIP entry
(Mar.)   B85-00322

Privatisation and the welfare state / Julian Le
Grand and Ray Robinson, editors. — London :
Allen & Unwin, 1984. — xiv,233p : ill ; 22cm
Bibliography: p212-224. — Includes index
ISBN 0-04-336079-3 (cased) : £18.00 : CIP rev.
ISBN 0-04-336080-7 (pbk) : £6.95   B84-24159

361.6'0941 — Great Britain. Public welfare
services. Long-range planning
A User's guide to the balance of care report. —
[London] : [Alexander Fleming House,
Elephant and Castle, SE1 6NY] / Arthur
Andersen in association with Operational
Research Service
Vol. 1: Non-technical user manual. — 1981. —
87p : ill ; 30cm
No price (unbound)   B85-04729

361.6'0983 — Chile. Community development
projects — *Case studies*
Richards, Howard. *1936-.* The evaluation of
cultural action : an evaluative study of the
Parents and Children Program (PPH) /
Howard Richards with the assistance of
Horacio Walker and Luis Brahm and the
advice of Juan-Eduardo Garcia-Huidobro,
Edmund V. Sullivan and Joel Weiss ; foreword
by Malcolm Parlett. — London : Macmillan in
association with International Development
Research Centre, 1985. — xx,246p ; 23cm. —
(Studies in international development research)
Includes index
ISBN 0-333-36338-8 (cased) : No price : CIP
rev.
ISBN 0-333-36339-6 (pbk) : No price
                                        B84-21074

361.6'1 — Regional planning
Weaver, Clyde. Regional development and the
local community : planning, politics and social
context / Clyde Weaver. — Chichester : Wiley,
c1984. — x,205p ; 24cm
Bibliography: p164-188. — Includes index
ISBN 0-471-90067-2 : £14.95 : CIP rev.
                                        B84-11363

361.6'1 — Social planning
The Fields and methods of social planning /
edited by James Midgley and David Piachaud.
— London : Heinemann Educational, 1984. —
vii,215p ; 23cm
Bibliography: p198-209. — Includes index
ISBN 0-435-82583-6 (cased) : No price
ISBN 0-435-82584-4 (pbk) : No price
                                        B85-01780

361.6'1'018 — Social planning. Spatial analysis
Recent developments in spatial data analysis :
methodology, measurement, models / [editors]
Gerhard Bahrenberg, Manfred M. Fischer,
Peter Nijkamp. — Aldershot : Gower, c1984.
— x,426p : ill,maps ; 23cm
Includes bibliographies
ISBN 0-566-00685-5 : £21.45 : CIP rev.
                                        B84-18844

361.6'1'094 — European Community. Social policies
New dimensions in European social policy /
edited by Jacques Vandamme. — London :
Croom Helm in association with the Trans
European Policy Studies Association, c1985. —
[224]p
Includes index
ISBN 0-7099-2473-9 : £16.95 : CIP entry
(Mar.)   B85-06272

361.6'1'0941 — Great Britain. Government. Social
policies, 1870-1914
Davidson, Roger. Whitehall and the labour
problem in late-Victorian and Edwardian
Britain : a study in official statistics and social
control / Roger Davidson. — London : Croom
Helm, c1985. — ix,293p ; 23cm
Bibliography: p281-284. — Includes index
ISBN 0-7099-0832-6 : £18.95 : CIP rev.
                                        B84-30508

361.6'1'0941 — Great Britain. Government. Social
policies, 1945-1981
Social policy and social welfare. — Milton
Keynes : Open University Press. — (Social
sciences : a third level course)
Block 1: Conflict and controversy over welfare
provision. — 1984. — 31p : ill ; 30cm. —
(D355 : block 1, unit 1)
At head of title: The Open University.
Bibliography: p31. — Contents: Unit 1 :
Welfare, conflict and controversy
ISBN 0-335-12170-5 (pbk) : No price
                                        B85-04645

Social policy and social welfare. — Milton
Keynes : Open University Press. — (Social
sciences : a third level course)
Block 1: Conflict and controversy over welfare
provision. — 1984. — 139p : ill,ports ; 30cm.
— (D355 : block 1, units 2-4)
At head of title: The Open University.
Includes bibliographies. — Contents: Unit 2:
Ideologies of welfare, the turn of the century
— Unit 3: Ideologies of welfare, the moment of
'1945' — Unit 4: Ideologies of Welfare, into
the 1980's
ISBN 0-335-12171-3 (pbk) : No price
                                        B85-04165

361.6'1'0941 — Great Britain. Social policies.
Decision making. Applications of social sciences
research
Thomas, Patricia. The aims and outcomes of
social policy research / Patricia Thomas. —
London : Croom Helm, 1985. — [128]p
Includes index
ISBN 0-7099-2492-5 : £12.95 : CIP entry
(Mar.)   B85-01393

361.6'1'094923 — Netherlands. Randstad. Regional
planning
Lawrence, G. R. P. Randstad Holland / G.R.P.
Lawrence. — Oxford : Oxford University
Press, 1973 (1979 [printing]). — 48p : ill,maps
(some col.) ; 25cm. — (Problem regions of
Europe)
Bibliography: p46. — Includes index
ISBN 0-19-913101-5 (pbk) : No price
                                        B85-09248

9 A sample page from the main classified sequence in *BNB*

listed in the schedules. Thus, to take a very simplistic example from the field of education, an enumerative classification scheme might first of all divide the subject field into a number of groups using a particular characteristic of the subject field such as level of education. This characteristic of the subject would then be used to divide out the whole of the field into a first array of subjects. Thus we would produce:

Primary
Secondary
Further
Higher

It is important that this first grouping of subjects is done exhaustively, because if we omit a particular concept at this early stage there will be major problems in the scheme at a later date. This first grouping is then subdivided by a second characteristic of the subject, possibly subject taught, giving an array of all the subjects taught in education which must subdivide each of the levels of education produced in the first grouping. Thus we will have an arrangement:

Primary
    Art
    History
    Geography
    etc.
Secondary
    Art
    History
    Geography
    etc.
Further
    Art
    History
    Geography
    etc.
Higher
    Art
    History
    Geography
    etc

A third characteristic of education might be the teaching method. This will produce an array of concepts including 'project work', 'seminar' and so on which must be used to divide each of the subjects taught that were produced by the division using the previous characteristic.

Thus we now have a schedule which runs as follows:

Primary
    Art
        project work
        seminar
    History
        project work
        seminar
    Geography
        project work
        seminar

Thus we can see that a schedule is slowly evolved by dividing a subject up into groups of related subjects using one particular characteristic of a subject. Each of these groups is then subdivided by a further array of subjects produced by another characteristic.

There are obviously a number of decisions involved in this process, particularly the choice of characteristics used to divide the subject; the order in which each characteristic is applied in the process of division and then the order of concepts in each of the resulting arrays. Thus in this case, if the subject taught had been the characteristic used in the initial process of division then each level of school would have been subarranged under all the various subjects.

A classification scheme will therefore group together the subjects that are the result of the first characteristic of division, whilst they will scatter subjects produced by subsequent characteristics. Thus in the example given the various subjects taught are scattered amongst all the types of schools, whilst teaching using project work in particular is scattered amongst all the subjects which are in turn scattered amongst all the various levels of education. This process of grouping and its corollary of scattering is always evident in the process of classification. The decision over which characteristics are chosen first is therefore crucial to the whole user orientation of a particular classification scheme. It is a problem that we shall term the citation order, and it will recur when we look at faceted classification schemes and all the other types of pre-coordinate indexing systems.

However, from this process we can see how the traditional enumerative classification schemes evolved, and when the Dewey decimal classification is discussed in the next chapter it can be seen how a particular classification scheme has developed. This enumerative process of producing schedules results in a reasonable working classification, and, although the traditional classification schemes did not follow this methodology in total, those main classes where it can be seen working are particularly successful.

Once the schedule has been produced then a notation is assigned to it; in the Dewey decimal classification's case it is a simple, expressive decimal notation using numbers, with each application of a characteristic of division resulting in a notation that is one digit longer. However, the particular problem of this enumerative approach is that the emergence of new concepts produces major difficulties. The arrival of a new type of school for example, requires not only space to be made in the level of education array, but all the subsequent subdivisions of subject taught and teaching methods have to be made.

Within this enumerative approach there are always certain over-riding generalist concepts such as time and geographical place which recur continuously throughout any subject. Theoretically, of course, such time and place subdivisions should be added on as a final characteristic and used to subdivide every single concept that exists in the schedules. Certain traditional bibliographic classification schemes, such as the Library of Congress classification adopt this approach. Common sense suggests that a neater solution to the problem would be to have certain numbers always meaning a particular time or a particular place which can then be added on to any other number in the schedule. This process of 'synthesis' can be seen in the Dewey decimal classification, where **0942** always means **Great Britain**, and can be added on, with a few exceptions, to any number in the schedule.

Similarly, physical form such as a periodical or an encyclopaedia is a concept which needs to be identified on certain occasions and should also be a piece of standard notation, such as 03 in the Dewey decimal classification to signify an encyclopaedia. It is this synthesis in an enumerative classification which allows an increased specificity in the vocabulary and therefore an increased level of precision for a particular user who needs to search for extremely detailed subjects.

Certain classification schemes, such as the Universal decimal classification discussed later, take this process of synthesis to an extremely high degree, allowing a wide range of numbers to be joined together to specify very precise concepts. From this process of increased synthesis emerged the alternative methodology for producing classification schemes.

Faceted classification schemes

Faceted classification schemes, technically called analytico-synthetic, reject this model of a process of division using characteristics with the resulting duplication of an idea such as **Art** or **History** throughout the schedule. Faceted classification schemes are produced by analysing the text and the terms used by searchers to identify single isolated terms which are then grouped together to form lists of related concepts, or foci within a broader category which is known as a facet. Thus, to return to our education example, we would produce;

Level of education	*Subject taught*	*Teaching method*
1 Primary	A Art	A Project work
2 Secondary	B History	B Seminar
3 Further	C Geography	
4 Higher		

We see emerging here three facets for: **level of education, subject taught** and **teaching method**. If we assign pieces of notation to each concept or focus in these facets then the individual foci can be gathered together from the relevant facets and the numbers joined together to form a classmark. Thus if we had assigned the numbers 1 2 3 4 to the **level of education** facet, and lower case a b c to the **subject taught** facet and capital letters A B to the **teaching method** facet then we could synthesize a classmark for **teaching art in secondary schools using projects** to give a number 2/2/A. Facets are thus groupings of terms of foci based on some characteristic of the subject. They are often groupings of materials, processes or people, but facets will differ from subject class to subject class. In social welfare, facets will be needed for problems, agencies and tactics as well as the usual facet for people.

In both the faceted and the enumerative classification scheme we were able to produce a number to indicate a particular concept. The key difference was that in the faceted classification scheme we synthesized the number by bringing the various foci together from different facets, whilst in the enumerative classification scheme the schedule actually listed the concept for **teaching art in secondary schools using projects.**

However, the vital difference is that if a new type of school or a new subject taught or a new teaching method is required in the schedules it is only necessary to insert the new concept into the relevant facet and all the other synthetic possibilities are instantly available. A large number of concepts to come about as new subjects interrelate with each other. If a faceted classification scheme exists for the whole of knowledge then new subjects can be classified simply by joining together concepts from facets which had hitherto never been linked. In an enumerative classification scheme this is less possible, as the schedule has actually to list concepts before they can be classified.

In a faceted classification scheme there are the same key decisions to be made as in the enumerative scheme but they are presented slightly differently. The decision over which characteristic to divide the subject up by is replaced by decision over which facets exist for each subject. In a faceted scheme we must make sure that we have all the relevant facets for every subject that is going to be required in the information unit. The decision over the order of the division by characteristics is replaced by an identical decision over the order which we shall use to join the numbers together from the various facets. Thus in a faceted classification scheme the citation order is determined by the decision about whether we will put **level of school,** followed by **subject taught** followed by **teaching method** when we synthesize the various concepts together from the three facets; or whether we might put **subject taught** first, followed by **teaching method,** followed by **level of school.** In either case we group all related concepts together from the facet that we cite first, and scatter concepts that come from the facet that we cite second.

This citation order is a fairly fundamental decision in a facet classification scheme, and unlike in an enumerative scheme it can be made by the information unit itself. Although all faceted classification schemes give an indicative citation order it is possible for a particular information unit to modify that order so that particular concepts are brought together. Thus, as we shall see in the next chapter, in the Bliss bibliographic classification scheme it is normal to cite the social problem first, followed by elements such as administration so that there is a grouping together of all persons in need. However, so that the very key concept **Social security and welfare payments** can be grouped together rather than being scattered amongst all the various types of need, the citation order can be modified so that in the particular instance of social security payments there is a grouping together of all these concepts. This ability for faceted classification schemes to allow citation orders to be modified by the information unit means that each unit may need to have a reasonably detailed knowledge of its own users' requirements so that sensible decisions on citation orders can be made.

Decisions are also necessary to determine the order of the various concepts in each facet. These decisions are identical to those concerned with the arrangement of concepts in the array for enumerative classification schemes. The designers of both types of schemes need to refer back continually to the various subject disciplines and the needs of users in order to come up with sensible solutions. As these decisions radically affect the type of arrangement that a user meets when searching they are obviously important.

It is the relevance of the various citation orders and orders of terms in each facet that affect whether or not an information unit adopts a particular classification scheme. When an information unit analyses a range of different classification schemes before deciding which one to adopt, it is this review of orders of terms in each facet and the particular facets identified, along with the suggested citation order, that should determine adoption or otherwise.

As we have seen in Chapter 1 increased specificity of an index language or classification scheme results in greater user precision or satisfactory retrieval of specific relevant items. Therefore a greater synthesis available within a classification scheme results in a higher precision for the searcher. Faceted classification schemes, being totally synthetic, tend to result in far higher levels of precision in the searching process. This is because few enumerative classification schemes are able to produce schedules that actually show the extremely detailed division required, simply because the size of the resulting schedules would make them impossible to handle. Thus the enumerative classification schemes that are available tend to be in the area of general bibliographic schemes for large academic or public libraries, or alternatively very early schedules in specialized

```
FOOD                                                641.3
   Contamination by microorganisms                  576.1'63
   Contamination by microorganisms - Conference
     proceedings                                     576.1'63
   Toxic effects of pesticide residues in food      614'.31
FOOD.  France                                       641.3'00944
FOOD.  Italy                                        641.3'00945
FOOD distribution trades.   Great Britain
          - Inquiry reports                          381'.45'641300942
FOOD manufacturing industries.   Great Britain       338.4'7'664002542
FOOD preservation.  Great Britain
 Cold storage.  National Federation of Cold
 Storage and Ice Trades - Yearbooks                  664'.02852'06242
FOOD storage buildings.   Ancient Rome
 Architectural features                              725'.35
```

10 Part of a subject index to a classified retrieval scheme

areas which are now starting to be modified along faceted lines. In one particular instance, the Bliss bibliographic classification, originally an enumerative classification, is now being modified to become a fully faceted one.

Subject indexes to the classified sequence

Because a classification scheme uses a notation to describe subject concepts, the resulting classmarks lack meaning; they require some sort of translation. Users will need an entry vocabulary or index, which lists all the words that they will need to search under and translates them into the notation of the classification scheme. This subject index (for an example see figure 10) will have no information about particular items but will merely list all the entry words a user may require for items that exist in the system, linking them to the classmarks. The various methods available for producing a subject index to a classified retrieval system are discussed in Chapter 5.

4 Some classification schemes

THE DEWEY DECIMAL CLASSIFICATION

The bibliographic classification scheme designed by Melvil Dewey in 1876 is one of the great traditional classification schemes used in libraries. Originally published as a 42-page work for a small college of higher education in America, it offered for the first time the ability to arrange books in a subject order that allowed differing levels of growth in different subject areas. Hitherto, particular shelves or bays in a library had been assigned subject marks and new additions could be added at the end of a sequence until each area was full. Once the library was full it became difficult to retain the subject arrangement. Dewey's concept of relative location, assigning a decimal notation to the items themselves and having the catalogue refer to the notation on the book rather than a number on the shelf, was revolutionary.

The classification scheme grew from its simple beginnings to a situation now in its 19th edition where it is used in the majority of public libraries both in England and America, along with a high proportion of academic libraries. This means that the understanding, training and general familiarization of librarians with the Dewey decimal classification is very strong indeed. Because the classification scheme has a beautifully simple notation, and is fairly straightforward to use, it is sometimes difficult for librarians brought up in the mainstream of the profession to conceive of any reasonable alternative. The process of training and familiarization for both librarians and users starts in schools, where a large number of school libraries use Dewey, in the abridged 11th edition.

It is the very simplicity of the classification scheme that has resulted in its popularity, and that popularity ensures that it continues to be used because of the resulting support in terms of training, co-operation and economies of scale.

Main class structure
Dewey divided the whole of knowledge into ten main classes, and then divided each of these into ten subdivisions and then each of the subdivisions into ten sections.

The main classes adopted by Dewey were:

000 Generalities
100 Philosophy and related discipline
200 Religion
300 Social sciences
400 Language
500 Pure sciences
600 Technology
700 The arts
800 Literature
900 General Geography and History

Dewey decimal is a discipline-oriented scheme, ie items are put in the main classes to which they are related through their broad parent discipline. Thus a concrete item such as a motorcar might appear in a number of different main classes depending on whether it is the design of motorcars, the manufacturing of motorcars, the management of motorcars or the social implications of motorcars that is being treated. It is important to grasp this, for if a classification scheme is to work the essential principles behind the relationships being shown need to be understood. In the case of Dewey that relationship is essentially one of showing academic discipline. This will of course cause problems when concrete items such as housing need to be looked at in detail and in Dewey the information will be scattered amongst the number of differing main classes. As we have seen, of course, this problem of certain things always being scattered is the cost of bringing other things together. The classification scheme tries to bring the items together that suit the majority of users, but there will always be some who find the arrangement counterproductive.

Certain of Dewey's main classes are very successful indeed whilst others are less successful. In a main class such as literature (800) we see a perfect example of a traditional enumerative classification working successfully. The concept Literature is broken down by the application of the subject characteristic Language, to produce an array of: **American literature 810, English literature 820, German literature 830, French literature 840 etc.** (see figure 11).

These subdivisions are then further divided by a second characteristic of physical form of material to give poetry, drama, novels, etc. as the subdivisions of each language. Each individual form of literature can then be subdivided by date so that **.1** means **Early English Period, .3** means the **Elizabethan Period** and **.8** means the **Victorian Period.** Thus as we look at the schedules we can produce a number such as **821.3** for **Elizabethan English Poetry.**

The notation is simple and expressive, with each extra digit meaning that the concept has been divided by a further characteristic producing another set of arrays. Thus **800** means **literature, 820** means **English literature, 821** means **English poetry** and **821.3** means **Elizabethan English poetry.** It is this simplicity which is so attractive. The fact that in the literature class **1** in the third digit place always means **poetry** ensures a high level of memorability or mnemonic qualities. Similarly, the fact that the subdivision after the decimal point normally means a time subdivision allows searchers to grasp easily the relationships between the various items in the literature class in an almost spatial way.

However, the literature class is a very traditional class which is fairly simple to arrange in a logical fashion. Moving to a class such as **Social problems and services** which in Dewey is at 360 throws up some of the major difficulties. The divisions of Social problems and services, instead of being broken down by the application of a formal subject characteristic such as type of problem, or type of person, has in fact been subdivided by a number of very different characteristics to produce an array which includes:

361 Social problems
362 Social welfare problems and services
363 Other social problems and services
364 Criminology
365 Penal institutions
366 Associations
367 General clubs
368 Insurance
369 Miscellaneous kinds of association

We see here a great hotch-potch of subdivisions, with a strong emphasis on criminology, penal problems and associations, clubs and

Literature (Belles-lettres)

800	Literature (Belles-lettres)	850	Italian, Romanian, Rhaeto-Romanic
801	Philosophy & theory	851	Italian poetry
802	Miscellany about literature	852	Italian drama
803	Dictionaries & encyclopedias	853	Italian fiction
804		854	Italian essays
805	Serial publications	855	Italian speeches
806	Organizations	856	Italian letters
807	Study & teaching	857	Italian satire & humor
808	Rhetoric & collections	858	Italian miscellaneous writings
809	History, description, critical appraisal	859	Romanian & Rhaeto-Romanic
810	American literature in English	860	Spanish & Portuguese literatures
811	Poetry	861	Spanish poetry
812	Drama	862	Spanish drama
813	Fiction	863	Spanish fiction
814	Essays	864	Spanish essays
815	Speeches	865	Spanish speeches
816	Letters	866	Spanish letters
817	Satire & humor	867	Spanish satire & humor
818	Miscellaneous writings	868	Spanish miscellaneous writings
819		869	Portuguese
820	English & Anglo-Saxon literatures	870	Italic literatures Latin
821	English poetry	871	Latin poetry
822	English drama	872	Latin dramatic poetry & drama
823	English fiction	873	Latin epic poetry & fiction
824	English essays	874	Latin lyric poetry
825	English speeches	875	Latin speeches
826	English letters	876	Latin letters
827	English satire & humor	877	Latin satire & humor
828	English miscellaneous writings	878	Latin miscellaneous writings
829	Anglo-Saxon (Old English)	879	Other Italic languages
830	Literatures of Germanic languages	880	Hellenic literatures Greek
831	German poetry	881	Classical Greek poetry
832	German drama	882	Classical Greek drama
833	German fiction	883	Classical Greek epic poetry
834	German essays	884	Classical Greek lyric poetry
835	German speeches	885	Classical Greek speeches
836	German letters	886	Classical Greek letters
837	German satire & humor	887	Classical Greek satire & humor
838	German miscellaneous writings	888	Classical Greek miscellaneous writings
839	Other Germanic literatures	889	Modern Greek
840	Literatures of Romance languages	890	Literatures of other languages
841	French poetry	891	East Indo-European & Celtic
842	French drama	892	Afro-Asiatic (Hamito-Semitic)
843	French fiction	893	Hamitic & Chad literatures
844	French essays	894	Ural-Altaic, Paleosiberian, Dravidian
845	French speeches	895	Sino-Tibetan & other Asian
846	French letters	896	African literatures
847	French satire & humor	897	North American native literatures
848	French miscellaneous writings	898	South American native literatures
849	Provençal & Catalan	899	Other literatures

Reproduced with the permission of Forest Press.

11 The main class 'Literature' from the Dewey decimal classification

insurance. The three vital subdivisions at **361, 362** and **363** (see figure 12) include a fairly random grouping of subdivisions which bring **public safety and hazards** in at **363.1** followed by **police** at **363.2** and **problems and controversy related to public morals** in at **363.4**. The latter includes issues such as **abortion** at **363.46, pornography** at **363.47** and **homosexuality** at **363.49**. The grouping of the last three indicates the problems that a traditional academic classification scheme has, when it is applied in an area where user demands might be very different. The grouping together of abortion, pornography and homsexuality as issues relating to public morals will cause enormous difficulties in many areas of community advice and information. The fact that it is followed directly at **363.5** by **housing** only makes the problem even more acute. Housing is one of the major issues in many areas of community information work and its brief allocation of notation, allied with very limited abilities for subdivision means that quite creative classification has to take place before the housing subdivision in Dewey can be used in many agencies.

Nonetheless, it has to be admitted at least that in Dewey there are blocks of notation for essential concepts, and they are recognized by user and librarian alike. The present edition, the nineteenth, was published in 1979, and a new edition is expected in 1986. The policy of the current editors of Dewey is one of revision and change, with the inclusion of totally rewritten 'phoenix' sections in a number of key main classes in each new edition. Thus, main classes such as law and mathematics will be completely recast and restructured. Over a long period of time it is anticipated that each major main class will eventually be totally restructured. The difficulty here is, of course, that each restructuring involves a library or information unit having to integrate its old stock with the old numbers into the new classification scheme. This will require some detailed re-classification at times, or, alternatively, a ruthless editing out and weeding of old stock to reduce the costs of reclassifying it. In many information units, this might be an excellent outcome.

Notation
The notation for the Dewey decimal classification is beautifully simple and pure. The notational base is 0–9, which is rather short and will therefore result in numbers being slightly longer than mixed notation classification schemes. The notation is also expressive,

363	Social problems and services; association	363

.378	Fire extinction services
.378 1	Rescue operations
.379	Fire hazards in specific situations

Examples: in transportation, in schools, in high-rise buildings

Class generalities of fire hazards in specific situations in 363.3701–363.3781

Problems and controversies related to public morals and customs

| .41 | Sale of alcoholic beverages |

Class problems of and services to alcoholics in 362.292

.42	Gambling
.44	Prostitution
.45	Drug traffic

Class problems of and services to drug addicts in 362.293

.46	Abortion
.47	Obscenity and pornography
.48	Pre- and extramarital relations

For prostitution, see 363.44

| .49 | Homosexuality |
| .5 | *Housing |

Class here interdisciplinary works on housing

Use of this number for public works discontinued; class in 363

Class a specific aspect of housing with the subject, e.g., sociological aspects 306.3, economic aspects 333.338

| .51 | Housing conditions |

Including discrimination in housing

| [.52] | Boundaries of problem |

Do not use; class in 363.51

| .58 | Programs and services |

Examples: rental subsidies, public housing, urban homesteading

Add as instructed under 362–363

12 Part of the Social problems and services schedule (363) from the Dewey decimal classification

which means that it will generally get longer by one digit at a time for each division of the subject. This also results in longer notation, but is very valuable for the user browsing through collections who can get a spatial feel for the extent of the subject discipline simply by looking at the length of the notation. Thus a sudden move up from a long number to a very short one allows users to see and feel that they have moved out of the area of initial enquiry into something else. This advantage must not be over-stressed. A good classification scheme should allow the user to grasp this point fully because of changes in the items that are examined rather than having to discover that the length of the notation has changed.

The classification scheme also has a number of useful notational devices. The 09 is used as a facet indicator for space and time, and can be added to the end of virtually all notation. This has a useful mnemonic value, as well as allowing detailed subdivision in the schedules where necessary. Similarly, 01 to 08 are common subdivisions for physical form, allowing one to specify that an item is a periodical or an encyclopaedia. These notational devices allow great specificity to be brought into operation where necessary, admittedly at the cost of longer numbers. Similarly, certain classmarks can be added to others in the schedules when even greater specificity is needed.

How to use the Dewey decimal classification

The classification scheme in its present edition is in three volumes; volume 1 for the introduction and common schedules, volume 2 the schedules themselves and volume 3 the index. Earlier editions were in two or single volumes. The present edition is obtainable from the Forest Press Lake Placid Education Foundation, Albany, New York, USA. Their English agents are Combridge Jackson. The cost of a full set of the present edition is £60.00. This is an expensive investment for many information units, and two alternatives exist. There is an abridged (11th) edition of Dewey, designed originally for school libraries which might be of interest to very generalized information units requiring little specificity in their retrieval system. Alternatively, second-hand sets of earlier editions may be available from libraries and library schools who no longer require them. Contacts through local public libraries or institutions of higher education within the area might find such second-hand editions. Again they really are of value only to those information units that are just setting up, have very few resources, and are looking at the possibility of using a general classification scheme such as Dewey and want to test this for a limited period before making final judgements.

Classification using Dewey decimal is reasonably straightforward, as long as the items fit primarily into an academic structure and no great specificity is required. Thus a subject such as 'a counselling service for drug addicts' is looked up in the index under the most specific concrete part of the concept. Under 'Addictive drugs' in the index (see figure 13) is a series of sub-headings showing the places in the main schedules where drugs and drug addiction are discussed. The area of 'counselling to drug addicts' appears in the Social science main class under the heading **Social problems** at **362.29386** (see figure 14).

The schedules allow some further subdivisions if necessary by use of a facet which can be applied to the whole of the social welfare class. This common facet is listed at the beginning of the class (see figure 15) and allows aspects such as **financial assistance 82** or **residential care 85** to be added on to the number. Thus if one has an

Drug			Addictive drugs	
abuse			use	362.293
programs			gen. med.	616.863
pers. admin.			geriatrics	618.976 863
gen. management	658.382 2		hygiene	613.83
spec. subj.	*s.s.*–068 3		pediatrics	618.928 63
pub. admin.	350.16		perinatal	618.326 8
central govts.	351.16		psychology	157.6
spec. jur.	353–354		soc. path.	362.293
local govts.	352.005 16		soc. theology *see* Social	
s.a. Addictive drugs use			problems soc. theology	
allergies			statistics	312.386 3
gen. med.	616.975		deaths	312.268 63
geriatrics	618.976 975		*other aspects see* Diseases	
pediatrics	618.929 75		Addicts *see spec. kinds e.g.*	
pub. health	614.599 3		Alcoholics	
statistics	312.397 5			
deaths	312.269 75			
other aspects see Diseases				
shock therapy *see* Shock				
(convulsions) therapy				
therapy	615.58			
dentistry	617.606 1			
ophthalmology	617.706 1			
otology	617.806 1			
psychiatry	616.891 8			
geriatrics	618.976 891 8			
pediatrics	618.928 918			

13 The entries for 'Drug' and 'Addictive drugs' from the index of the Dewey decimal classification

▶   **362.21–362.28 Medical care**

Class comprehensive works in 362.2, medical treatment in 616.8, care of the addicted in 362.29

.21   Services of psychiatric hospitals and related institutions

For services of psychiatric clinics, see 362.22; of sanitariums and nursing homes, 362.23

.22   Services of psychiatric clinics

.23   Services of sanitariums and nursing homes

.24   Home care

Emergency services

Including "hot lines"

.29   Addictions

.292   *Alcoholism

[.292 6]   Control of sale of alcoholic beverages

Do not use; class in 363.41

[.292 7]   Prevention

Do not use; class in 362.29286

.292 8   Services to alcoholics

.292 86   Counseling, guidance, education

Example: services of Alcoholics Anonymous

Including prevention of alcoholism

.293   *Drug addiction

[.293 6]   Control of drug traffic

Do not use; class in 363.45

93 7]   Prevention

Do not use; class in 362.29386

.293 8   Services to drug addicts

.293 86   Counseling, guidance, education

Including prevention of addiction

.3   *Mental retardation

*Add as instructed under 362–363

14 Another part of the Social problems and services schedule (362) from the Dewey decimal classification

▶ **362–363 Specific social problems and services**

Except for additions, changes, deletions, exceptions shown under specific entries, add to each subdivision identified by * as follows:

01	Philosophy and theory
02	Miscellany
028	Techniques, procedures, apparatus, equipment, materials
[0289]	Safety measures
	Do not use; class in 75
03–09	Standard subdivisions
	Notations from Table 1
▶1–3	Characteristics of problem
	Class comprehensive works in base number
1	Social causes
2	Boundaries
	Extent, distribution, severity, incidence
3	Social effects
5	Social action
	To alleviate specific problems, for the relief of specific classes of persons
	Add to 5 the numbers following 361 in 361.2–361.8, e.g., international action 526
	Class specific forms of action in 6–8
▶6–8	Specific forms of action
	Class comprehensive works in 5
6	Control
	Elimination and reduction of hazards, of sources and causes of difficulty
62	Standards
63	Monitoring, surveillance, reporting
64	Inspection and testing
65	Investigation of specific incidents
66	Certification
7	Prevention
	Measures to prevent ill effects, to preclude operation of existing hazards, of existing sources and causes of difficulty
	Class here preparedness
72	Protective measures
	Design of environments, warning and guidance systems, equipment to diminish likelihood of untoward effects
75	Safety measures
	Operative practices, techniques of performing activities in such a manner as to diminish likelihood of untoward effects
8	Remedial measures, services, forms of assistance
	Class social work in 53
81	Rescue operations
82	Financial assistance
	Class social insurance in 368.4
83	Direct relief
	Including provision of food, shelter, household assistance, clothing, recreation, other material necessities, e.g., hearing aids
	For employment services, see 84; residential care, 85
84	Employment services
	Including vocational rehabilitation, sheltered employment
85	Residential care
	Care within institutions existing for the purpose
86	Counseling and guidance

Class comprehensive works in 361, discrimination in 305

For criminology, see 364

15 Example of a specialist facet from the Dewey decimal classification class 362–363

extensive collection on drug addiction then more detailed sub-arrangement using this common facet is possible. The fact that such common facets exist throughout Dewey is indicated by an asterisk and an 'add note' on the relevant page. There is an example at 'Housing' in figure 12 and several more in figure 14. This facility only exists in certain places in the schedules, generally in areas of poor specificity where greater detail is slowly being inserted into the schedule.

Once a place and a number have been found in the schedules a decision can be made on whether or not subdivision is needed into place, time or physical form. These possibilities are important when extensive collections are being built up in certain areas and greater detail is required to break the collections down to more user-friendly arrangements.

Place can be added to most numbers in Dewey directly by the use of the 09 indicator. Thus **094248** indicates **Birmingham**, and a geographical breakdown on counselling services to drug addicts by place would give a number **362.29386094248** to indicate **counselling to drug addicts in Birmingham.** These area table numbers are taken from the area tables listed in volume one of the classification scheme. These area tables are detailed, with a strong American bias to them. They tend to make all the numbers much longer than many users are prepared to accept, but they do allow more detailed breakdown in areas where collections have become large or a place is a vital aspect of the subject.

Similarly, numbers can be broken down by a physical form approach, which covers elements such as encyclopaedias, year books, programmed texts or audio-visual media. These physical-form breakdowns also enable aspects such as theory, education and training, associations and organizations, or even careers work, etc. to be indicated in the notation. These physical forms subdivisions are listed in table one of the common subdivisions in the first volume of classification scheme, and are all preceded with a zero. Thus 01 means the theory of the subject as opposed to the more practical applied aspects.

Problems with Dewey
The Dewey decimal classification is a general classification scheme, designed for libraries with collections that span most of the field of knowledge. It therefore does not provide the detail and specificity

required in many of the individual areas that information units have to specialize in. Because the notation base is fairly short all classification numbers tend to become long when the common subdivisions or special facets are applied.

The classification scheme is also designed primarily for academic collections with an arrangement and series of relationships that mirror the interests of academic libraries in America in the 1870s. It is thus accused of being biased towards American, white, Anglo-Saxon, protestant, middle-class, male communities that are often not relevant to the needs of many information units today.

However, there are certain major advantages to Dewey that cannot be ignored. Firstly it is there. This means that schedules can be acquired quickly. Most users, through their schooling or their use of the public library system, have some understanding of what the notation means, as will the majority of information workers whether trained or not. The fact that the scheme is used in local library systems also means that advice, technical support and possibly some co-operative advantages can be obtained. Reading lists and bibliographies produced by other information units will be usable within your own unit and the fact that there is an editorial system producing updated new editions means that change and improvement is always taking place. For a number of information units, especially those with a strong library slant, these advantages can outweigh the very serious disadvantages that Dewey provides in terms of subject specificity, subject relationships and the inability of the user to stand back and visualize subject links in a way that matches their requirements. It is true that these failings do not exist in all of the classes and subdivisions of Dewey, but they do in a large number.

Information units interested in adopting the Dewey decimal classification will obviously need to test it carefully by analysing the schedules in relation to their own information materials and users, and identifying those areas where the system fails. These failings can be overcome either by modifying the schedules in-house to give greater detail or by providing detailed instruction to both users and classifiers on how to understand and respond to some of the failings. Thus the paucity of detail in a number such as **363.5** for the **social problems of housing** will result in an information unit providing an in-house range of subdivisions, possibly building on a special facet that is provided for all social welfare problems.

It has to be recognized that the Dewey decimal classification was a brilliant concept for arranging books on shelves, and that its use in the majority of public and academic libraries ensures its continued support and development for many years ahead. However, the fact that it was designed in the 1870s, for small American college libraries to arrange their books by, means that it is sometimes difficult to adapt it in information-handling units whose prior commitment may not be towards book stock.

THE UNIVERSAL DECIMAL CLASSIFICATION
Rather later than Melvil Dewey, in 1894, two European documentalists, Paul Otlet and Henry Lafontaine, became interested in the idea of a 'Universal Index to recorded knowledge', to be available to the whole world. The international nature of this endeavour meant that Otlet and Lafontaine were attracted to the idea of a retrieval system that cut across the problems of language. Classification schemes, of course, do this. Their use of an arbitrary notation which has no bearing on the words used for that concept in different languages is irresistibly attractive. The use of a pure simple Arabic notation would make this task even easier. Thus, Otlet and Lafontaine approached Melvil Dewey for permission to use the notational structure of his decimal classification. However, far greater detail was needed for arranging a worldwide universal index to recorded knowledge, and therefore it needed a more extended version of decimal classification.

The resulting scheme, the Universal decimal classification (UDC) was published in French over the years 1927 to 1933 and was by far the most detailed classification scheme published at that time. German and English editions were started during the 1930s, and the full English edition has now been completed, published in separate pamphlet parts for all the various divisions and sub-divisions of the main classes. This is published by the British Standards Institution, the official British editorial body for the Universal decimal classification. BSI produce an abridged edition of UDC in hard-cover format, and a medium-sized edition was published in 1984. There is a very interesting trilingual edition published in 1958, which covers German, English and French on the same page.

Main classes and schedules
The original main class structure of UDC faithfully followed

Dewey's main classes. However, strong criticisms of this main class order during the 1960s resulted in main class 4 (language) being moved to join literature at main class 8, thus freeing main class 4 for future development. An early change was the dropping of the Dewey decimal convention that the main classes start in hundreds, with subdivisions moving down from that. In the Universal decimal classification each main class is allocated a single Arabic numeral; thus technology is 6. This results in a reduction of the length of number in the main class areas.

Thus the main class structure is as follows:

0 Generalities
1 Philosophy, metaphysics, psychology, logic, ethics and morals
2 Religion and theology
3 Social sciences, economics, law, government, education
4
5 Mathematics and natural sciences
6 Applied sciences, medicine and technology
7 The arts, recreation, sport
8 Literature, belle lettres, theology, linguistics, languages
9 Geography, biography and history

The classification scheme is published in both a single-volume, abridged edition which is British Standard 1000a, and also in fully detailed pamphlet parts that are called fascicules. There are more than 100 such fascicules, each one covering a particular part of the main schedules. Most information units obtain the relevant detailed fascicules for their disciplines, and then use the abridged schedules to provide classmarks for fringe material. Such a process allows each information unit to have detailed schedules for the relevant areas, without having to waste time and money on the detail in other areas.

UDC's scheme aims to produce a classmark which is a detailed synthesis of the subject content of each item in the system. While Dewey allows a summary of the major concept of each item by assigning one or possibly two classmarks which relate to what the item is mainly about, UDC allows a much more detailed analysis of the wide-ranging ideas within a particular item. In order to do this the classification scheme is very synthetic. Classmarks can be built up from various parts of the classification scheme to give a detailed resumé using numbers from different parts of the schedules, joined together with a range of punctuation marks that all imply subtly different relationships. For example **362:333.3(4248)** means **Social welfare and housing in Birmingham.**

Thus in the social welfare schedules of UDC at 362 (see figure 16) the array is based on the characteristics of people served and institution. These concepts can then be further divided by other problems and techniques brought from elsewhere in the schedules and linked to the original number by punctuation marks indicating the relationship.

Thus the plus sign + can be used to join two notation marks together if the document discusses two separate concepts. For example **Mining and Metallurgy**, results in the number **622+669.** The oblique stroke / is used to join the first and last of a series of consecutive UDC numbers showing a range of concepts which between them form a broad subject or branch of knowledge for which no single number exists. Thus **civil engineering 624/628.**

The relation sign : is the most powerful connecting symbol in UDC, and is used to link two or more UDC numbers whose concepts show some sort of relationship with each other. For example the array at **333.3** in UDC denotes **private property** (see figure 17) with a range of **problems** at **333.32** including **Tenants' and landlords' rights** at **333.323**; these can be joined to numbers in the **362 social welfare** area with a colon, allowing social welfare to be subdivided by a range of housing problems, eg. **362: 333.32 for social welfare problems of landlords' and tenants' rights.** The colon in UDC effectively allows any number to be subdivided or subarranged by any other number.

In the catalogue each item would probably be entered under all the various parts of the number that are joined together by a colon. This process is known as cycling, and allows the user to consult the classified catalogue at any part of the number that is relevant. Obviously, each information unit would have to decide which part of the number would be used to arrange the items in the physical store or on the shelves. The number cited first in the classmark on the item itself, under which it would be filed, would obviously be the most important aspect of that document for the information unit. Thus a decision would have to be made about whether the item **362:333.3** for **social welfare aspects of housing** would go under **social welfare** or **housing.** This decision on the citation order needs to be thought through carefully by the information unit.

362	SOCIAL WELFARE. Services, institutions, establishments, etc. *Cf.* 351.84; 725.5
(100)	International work, U.N.R.R.A.
.1	Medical (health) services. *Cf.* 361.1; 61
.11	Hospitals, infirmaries, etc.
.12	Clinics, dispensaries. *Cf.* 613/614
.13	Sanatoria, preventoria, spas
.14	Home nurses, visiting, etc.
.15	Maternity welfare. *Cf.* 618.2
.16	After-care, convalescence
.17	Family welfare. *Cf.* 331.226; 362.7
.178	Family planning. *Cf.* 613.88
.18	Aid in accident or injury cases
.191	Aid to wounded in wartime. Red Cross
.193	Social work in connection with disease, epidemics, etc. Cancer, T.B., V.D.
.2	Care of (certified) insane, lunatics. *Cf.* 343.816
.3	Welfare of feeble-minded, imbeciles, including backward and maladjusted children
.4	Welfare of physically handicapped
.41	Blind. *Cf.* 371.9
.42	Deaf. Deaf and dumb. *Cf.* 371.9
.5	Welfare of destitute, poor and needy. *Cf.* 331.6; 339.1
.52	Lodgings, hostels, doss-houses, etc.
.53	Money, seasonal allowances, winter help
.54	Help in kind, *e.g.* CARE (73–87)
.58	War victims. *Cf.* 355.292
.6	Welfare of the aged, infirm and sick
.61	Homes. Pensioners' homes
.62	Pensions, allowances. Old age pensions
.7	Child welfare: care, adoption, etc.
.71	Infant welfare. Homes. Crèches. *Cf.* 362.15
.72	Illegitimate children, waifs. Foundling homes
.73	Orphans. Orphanages
.74	Care, education and protection of neglected children. *Cf.* 179.2; 343.88
.75	Foster-child and -parent system
.76	School welfare, meals, etc. *Cf.* 371
.78	Care of sick children. Holiday settlements
.8	Youth welfare, clubs, etc. (boys and girls). *Cf.* 369.4
9	Social works, services, etc., for other categories
.92	Welfare of foreigners, refugees, etc.
.93	Welfare of the forces, prisoners of war: clubs, canteens, etc.
.94	Welfare of the middle-classes, new poor, victims of economic crises
.96	Provision for funerals. Interment, burial funds. *Cf.* 334.8; 362.6
.97	Social work on behalf of the unemployed. *Cf.* 331.6

Reproduced with the permission of the British Standards Institution.

16 The Social welfare schedules of the Universal decimal classification

333.3	**Private property. Housing problem, etc.**
.31	Family estate or seat. Homestead
.32	Housing problem.
	Cf. 334.1; 351.778.5; 69; 711; 728.1
.322	Housing reform: shortage, allocation, etc.
.323	Tenants' and landlords' rights; redress
.324	Compulsory letting. Commandeering
.325	Temporary, emergency housing
.326	Defective, condemned houses
.327	Housing sites, building land
.328	Gardens, allotments. *Cf.* 635
.33	Mortgages. *Cf.* 332.72; 347.27
.37	Large-scale ownership. Latifundia
.38	Small-scale property. Small holdings.
.39	Operations and speculations in land
.4	Property of absentees and foreigners.
.5	Agricultural property, land leased for farming
.6	Urban property
.7	Forest lands and property
.8	Property in mines, in subsoil
.9	Other forms of property. Water.
	Hunting and fishing property

Reproduced with the permission of the British Standards Institution.
17 The array Private property in the Universal decimal classification

Occasionally, concepts are joined together to describe an item where the second aspect is very minor and does not necessitate any extra entry to be made in the catalogue. For these instances a double colon is used, and indicates a relationship where the second part of the concept is very subsidiary and does not justify a separate entry in the catalogue.

The use of the colon and double colon in UDC can allow sophisticated strings of terms to be built up identifying the subject content of items very precisely. Allied to the ability to make catalogue entries under each part of the classmark, allowing possibly five or six separate entries in the classified catalogue, this results in a very valuable retrieval tool for the searcher.

However, UDC is still essentially a traditional, enumerative classification scheme, and the orders of concepts given in the schedules are sometimes not that successful. When concepts are joined with a colon the faults are compounded, especially when the colon has to be used to join very different concepts in very different relationships. If the order of concepts in a particular part of the schedules is unsatisfactory, then obviously that problem will be duplicated throughout the classified arrangement whenever that array of concepts is joined to any other number.

It is also true that the resulting numbers from this process of synthesis are extraordinarily long. This may not matter when the level of user satisfaction is raised by the resulting specificity, but it can matter a great deal when the orders and arrangements the searchers find is not particularly successful.

UDC also contains a wide range of other devices, termed common auxiliaries, that allow even further detail and specification. These common auxiliaries are not unlike the standard subdivisions found in Dewey, but take the idea of common facets applicable to the entire classification scheme to a much more detailed conclusion.

Common auxiliaries of form cover the physical forms of material, and are joined to numbers using brackets. Thus (05) indicates that the work is a **periodical publication,** and (063) indicates that the work is a **conference document.** This range of physical form indicators can be added to any other number in the schedules.

The common auxiliaries of place are similar to the area tables in Dewey. Thus (42) indicates **Britain** and (73) indicates the **United States.** A work that looks at the relationship between social problems in America and their impact on the social problems in Great Britain could be shown by 362(42:73). If necessary, entries can be made in the classified catalogue under both or either of the place auxiliaries, allowing searchers to be specific and, for example, to lift out aspects of a problem in America.

The common auxiliaries of race and nationality allow particular races and nationalities to be identified in texts. They use the language facets, and are shown by (=). Thus (=924) indicates a particular aspect of a subject in relation to the Jews.

The time auxiliary is one of the most interesting auxiliaries in UDC from a notational point of view. The facet indicator is " " and the date is put inside. Thus the classmark for a concept in 1984 simply has "1984" added to it, eg **social policy in 1984 362"1984".**

An interesting common auxiliary is the point-of-view facet. This is indicated by a . 00 and allows concepts to be split up by particular broad points of view. Thus 007 indicates the **manpower and personnel problem point of view,** whilst 005 indicates the **equipping and insulation problems** of any particular subject. A modification to the point-of-view facet is the ability to indicate the author's point of

view. This is 000 followed by a number from the rest of the classification scheme, allowing for example 000.335.5 to show the **Marxist point of view of the author.** Thus **social welfare from a Marxist
point of view** could be shown by 362.000.335.5.

It can be seen from this range of devices and auxiliaries that the
Universal decimal classification, has evolved to become a powerful
and sophisticated classification scheme for retrieval. The difficulties
are that its notation can become extraordinarily cumbersome,
especially when a large number of the common auxiliaries are used.
This problem is one of both filing and retrieval, with decisions on
filing orders and citation orders having to be understood by both the
classifier and the searcher. However, when searchers feel that the
gains to the retrieval process in terms of precision and relevance are
obviously clear then problems over length of notation can be borne.
The other problem with UDC is the strong technological bias of
the classification scheme. Much time and effort has been put into the
revision and updating procedures, many of them being based on
agreed experiences across a number of key libraries. Such libraries
tend to be in the areas of technology, science and management with
less involvement in the areas of social sciences and the humanities.

How to classify using the Universal decimal classification
Classifying using UDC is the same process of analysis, consultation
and synthesis that applies to all classification schemes. However, in
comparison with Dewey, the process is rather more complex. It is
also made more difficult by the fact that most information units will
have a number of separate fascicules for their various subject
interests, along with the abridged or medium-sized edition for their
more generalist material.

Because the classification scheme allows far more detailed synthesis, or number building, the process of analysis of the subject content of items needs to be rather more detailed. Concepts are checked
in the index to identify notation in the schedules. The schedules are
then consulted to check for further more detailed subdivisions or
notes or instructions about possible number use. Thus the example
on the social welfare problems of aspects of housing would identify
a number of possible subdivisions of housing at 333.3 covering the
various aspects of the problem. Issues such as **squatting** might be
placed in a number of places, including **commandeering** and
tenants' and landlords' rights. The fascicules for this part of the

schedules would give more detailed numbers than the abridged or medium-sized edition. If the item was on particular social welfare and legal problems then a decision would be made on whether to join it to numbers from the **362 social welfare** area as well as the **343.7 offences against property** array in the law class. The result of this process would be the synthesis of several parts to form a composite classmark for the item, eg **362 : 333.32 : 343.7**. On to these concepts could be added pieces of notation from the common auxiliaries to indicate place, time or particular point of view. A decision would then need to be made on the particular order in which the information unit wanted the various parts of the number. This order would depend on the previously decreed citation order that was operating within the information unit. A decision would already have been made on whether housing precedes legal problems which precedes social welfare problems or some alternative order.

This decision affects both the arrangement of items in the system and the subarrangement of items within the classified catalogue. For, even though we will make multiple entries under each part of the classmark in the classified catalogue, it will not be possible to permutate every single part of the number in every single possible combination because that would result in an enormous number of entries. If there are five parts to our UDC classmark, we shall normally only want to make entries under the five different parts of the classmark. The order in which we put the parts of the classmark are therefore important, for if we decide to cite **housing** first, followed by **law** and then by **social welfare**, social welfare problems will tend to be scattered within the concrete things to which they relate. Alternatively, if we decide to collocate all our material at **social welfare problems** subdivided by **housing** and then by **law**, the ability to retrieve everything under **law** becomes more difficult. However, a fixed citation order within the system is essential and the information unit will have to decide which facets, arrays and main classes are important for the users.

Thus from our consultation of the schedules, and decisions on the use of common auxiliaries, allied with the previous decision on citation order, the UDC classmark for the item is produced. It may be slightly more time-consuming than classifying using Dewey, for different parts of the classification scheme need to be consulted and decisions made on what relationships will be shown. Nonetheless, the resulting classmark is detailed and fairly specific and shows the spread of concepts that the item is trying to discuss. The resulting classmark will be long. UDC numbers will tend to be longer than Dewey numbers, for the scheme is used in order to get the specificity of vocabulary and therefore precision in a user's searching.

Once the classmark is produced then a system of producing the multiple access points needs to be followed. This can be achieved using multiple copies of cards or slips, printed or typed out with the full classmark along the top. Each part of the classmark can then be underlined in turn, and the card filed under each of the underlined parts of the mark. Thus 333.323:343.74:362.97, which might be an item discussing the **relationship between social services, the unemployed, squatting and trespass against private housing** might be entered in the catalogue in three places, with the full classmark written on top of each of three cards and the three parts underlined in turn to show the filer and the searcher why it is in each part of classified catalogue, thus:

333.323:343.74:362.97

333.323:343.74:362.97

333.323:343.74:362.97

From this process it can be seen that the user can go into the classified sequence of the catalogue at any of these three places and have the opportunity to pick up the relevant item. An alternative way of laying out this entry is to retype it, actually changing the order of the classmark each time so that the filing component of the number comes to the front and is followed by the other two components. This process is technically called cycling.

Obviously, as classification marks become more and more complex the need for a detailed subject index that will allow the user to look up the actual words or terms that are relevant to the inquiry and have them translated into the classmarks becomes all-important. This process of subject indexing will be discussed in more detail in Chapter 5 but the complexity of UDC requires extremely detailed subject indexing to the classified sequence if the advantages of cycling and multiple access points are to be fully realized.

Aids for the classifier

As part of the British Standards Institution publication programme for UDC there is British Standard BS1000C:1963 *Initial guide to the Universal decimal classification*, compiled by Jack Mills. This is an extremely valuable practical tool for users of UDC, and is also a very interesting blend of theory and practice on classification in general.

Because the Universal decimal classification is an official British Standard the abridged schedule of 1961, the medium-sized edition of 1984 as well as all the detailed fascicules are obtained from the British Standards Institution.

THE BLISS BIBLIOGRAPHIC CLASSIFICATION

The bibliographic classification of Henry Bliss was produced after much theoretical writing between 1946 and 1953. The bibliographic classification probably had more work put into its main class order and principles of division than any other traditional bibliographic scheme. Its use by libraries is limited, with only some 80 libraries in total adopting it. The lack of any major editorial and publishing body, along with rather dated subdivisions in many areas, resulted in the scheme being of great theoretical interest but of little practical value.

All this was transformed with the decision to produce a second edition in fully faceted form under the editorial direction of Jack Mills. It is this second edition which is of such great interest. Although not all the main classes are yet published a number of the key ones are, in particular class Q for social welfare. This main class has already been adopted in a number of libraries specializing in the areas of society and welfare, such as the Tavistock Institute.

Main classes and schedules

The main class structure of the Bliss bibliographic classification is of particular interest to information units in the areas of social science, social welfare and education. Bliss was keenly interested in the basic order of classes and identified principles on which such an order could be based, resulting in what he felt was a recognizable scientific and educational consensus.

A   Philosophy and general science
AM   Mathematics
AZ   Physical sciences

B	Physics
C	Chemistry
D	Astronomy
DG	Space sciences
DH	Earth sciences
E	Biology
F	Botany
G	Zoology
H	Anthropology
HM	Medicine
I	Psychology
J	Education
K	Social sciences
L	History
P	Religion (alternative at Z)
Q	Social welfare
R	Political science
S	Law
T	Economics
U	Technology
V	Aesthetic arts
W	Philology: language and literature
Z	Religion, occult, morals

The first edition was published as one multi-volume work but the second faceted edition is being published slowly over a period of time, with the main classes of anthropology, human biology, medicine, sociology, education, religion, social welfare, political science and law and economics all published already. The main classes that are of major interest to information units within the community and social welfare area are thus all in existence in a fully faceted edition.

In the social welfare class Q the facets are:

a) Persons in need (for example children, handicapped persons, delinquents): (QG – QT)
b) Causes of need (poverty, unemployment, illness): (QG – QT)
c) Forms of aid (care, grants, counselling): (QE – QF)
d) Methods, techniques in giving aid (social work, case work, interviewing, etc.): (QD)

e) Agents, instruments in social work (people, organizations): (QAU – QCV)
f) Principles of social welfare (policy, social administration): (QAB)
g) Common facets (place, time, form, etc.): (2 – 9)

Each facet is a group of concepts, and the notation is synthesized with the key facets of cause and need always being cited first. In the **persons in need** facet there will thus be a number of arrays such as members of the family, shown at QG – QT, where there are arrays grouped by kinship or by marital status (see figure 18). To these can be synthesized concepts such as counselling, to give **QMN LE** for **the counselling of disturbed children.**

A classification scheme of this sort is dependent on the process of synthesis, or building numbers up from the constituent foci in the various facets. This means that there need to be some basic rules on the order in which the numbers are built up – the citation order. If we have a concept such as **legal aid for one-person families** the two concepts that are relevant exist at **QEQS** in the **social services** area, and **QKT** in the **persons in need** facet. In this classification scheme the most important facet is regarded as a **persons in need** facet, and therefore **QKT** is cited first followed by **QEQS**. Because Q is the main classmark it need not be repeated when notation is synthesized, thus the classmark becomes **QKT EQS**.

The schedules are in a general to specific order, and so when we have an item with two pieces of notation we require that the item is placed at the more specific piece of notation followed by the more general. Thus we want our item on **legal aid for single-parent families** to go with **single-parent families** at **QKT**, subdivided by **EQS**. The rule in Bliss is therefore that whenever two pieces of notation are joined together the piece of notation that comes later in the schedules is always put first and is then followed by the piece of notation that comes from earlier on in the schedules. This device is called 'retroactive notation' and ensures that the citation order is always adhered to.

Common auxiliaries

As in all general classification schemes there needs to be some device for allowing form, space, time and other generalized concepts to be added to the notation. In Bliss the common subdivisions of form,

```
QG          PERSONS IN NEED, CAUSES OF NEED
QGG            Disadvantaged persons in general
QGH               Characteristics: physical, psychological,
                     social...
                  (Types of persons)
                     * If defined by aid received see
                       latter (e.g. Persons in care QEL):
                       if defined by cause of need see
                       latter (e.g. The Poor with
                       Poverty)
                  (Defined by events, conditions)
QGN                  Disasters, disaster relief
QGP                  Deprivation, poverty, unemployment
QH                Housing, accommodation
QJD               Victims of cruelty, violence,
                     discrimination...
                  (By other characteristics)
QJM                  Religion... sex... race...
QJG                  Civil/political status:
                        Immigrants...
QJW               Slaves
QK                (By family relationships) The Family
QKK               Size of family, family planning
                  (Members)
QKL Y                Single, unmarried
QKN                  Married, marriage: wives,
                        husbands
QKP                  Parents: mothers, fathers,
                        offspring
                  (Types of families)
QKS B                Families with dependents
QKT                  One parent families
QKU                  With special categories of
                        members
QKV                  With handicapped members
                  (Persons by age)
QL             Minors, children
QLL K             Adopted, fostered
QLV            Elderly, aged
QM           Physically or mentally disadvantaged
QMM            Mentally disadvantaged
QMN               Disturbed, emotionally disturbed
QMP            Handicapped mentally
QMQ          Physically disadvantaged
QMT            Handicapped, physically disabled:
                  blind ...
```

Reproduced with the permission of the Bliss Classification Association and
Butterworths.

18 Part of the Social welfare class (Q) in the Bliss bibliographic classification

time and place, along with the ability to specify types of relationships with other subjects such as 'comparison' and 'the influence'
are listed in the common auxiliary schedules in the first volume of
the classification scheme. Because they are the most generalized concepts of approach they come first in the schedules and therefore
come last when numbers are synthesized together. They can either
be added directly or through a facet indicator depending on the
common auxiliary involved. **Place**, for example, is listed in the
common auxiliary schedule two and is added to the number using
the facet indicator **8**. Thus our example on **legal aid for one-parent
families**, if taking place in **America**, would result in a classmark of
QKTEQS8Y. (Y being the notation for the USA).

Bliss is one of the most flexible of all schemes in that the classifier
is allowed far greater choice of alternative arrangements. The classification scheme indicates preferred alternatives but still allows the
classifier to reject or modify these alternatives. An excellent example
is in **social security QF** where there are two alternatives. Firstly, it is
possible to reject the normal citation rule of putting **person in need**
first followed by the **social security** notation. The scheme suggests
the classifier arranges all of the **social security to particular individuals** at the **QFD** number for **social security** by reversing the
normal retroactive notation. This means that each information unit
can decide whether to retain the normal **person in need** followed by
social welfare solution citation order or to reverse it and have all the
social security together at **QFD** with a subarrangement for all
people in need. This is a simple reversal of the normal citation order
for a particular place in the classification scheme.

Similarly, the normal decisions on place coming after concepts is
modified in the **social security** area at **QF** where place is such an integral part of the social security legislation that it is actually built into
the schedules at **QFQ**, so that numbers for particular parts of the
world can come before particular problems.

These two examples are indicative of the way that Bliss is striving
to allow individual information units to have some degree of auton-
omy over the design of their retrieval systems in relation to their
own particular users.

How to use the Bliss bibliographic classification
Bibliographic classification is rather like UDC in that there is a
number of separate volumes, each with its own index. The dif-

ference is, however, that Bliss does not yet have the general index that exists in UDC's abridged or medium-sized schedules. Thus to use Bliss effectively one needs to know the main class in which the item which is being classified should appear. However, in specialized information units this is not a great problem in that the relevant main class volumes from Bliss will most likely have been bought and decisions made on the relevance of the main classes. Thus, if an information unit is working from inside the **social welfare area** it will be using class **Q**, with possible additions from the **law** or **education** classes.

The classification process therefore starts with normal 'concept analysis' of the particular item, and means that the classifier has to recognize the relevant concepts in each item, and analyse them in terms of the facets that exist within the classification scheme. Each of the analysed concepts is then consulted in the index at the end of the schedules in order to identify the places in the facets where the concepts occur. Thus to classify a pamphlet on the problem of rent arrears for single-parent families the classifier would begin by identifying the different concepts involved (concept analysis). In this case they are **rent arrears** and **one-parent families**. Having identified the concepts they are looked up in turn in the index. **One-parent families** is shown in the index to be at **QKT** in the schedules. The concept **rent arrears** will be identified in the index under **arrears, rent** at **QHQRO**, or can be identified under the broader term **rents** at **QHQ** which can then be followed down to the more specific concept in the schedules themselves. The composite problem of **rent arrears for single-parent families** can then be synthesized resulting in the classmark **QKTHQRO**.

In summary, the Bliss bibliographic classification is a good example of a faceted scheme which is detailed but fairly simply used and which results in a pleasing and short notation. The fact that it is more than simply a specialist classification in subjects like social welfare, but has main classes in most of the other areas of the academic disciplines will obviously be very valuable to information units that might be diversifying into new emerging disciplines. However, not all the main classes are out yet and the level of detail given in the schedules is sometimes rather thin. Nonetheless, the scheme is a very positive example of subject retrieval within the social sciences. It is supported by the Bliss Classification Association which ensures the development of the scheme and produces the Bliss

Classification Bulletin. The classification scheme itself is available from Butterworths, 88 Kingsway, London WC2 and the Bliss Classification Association is based at the Commonwealth Institute, Kensington High Street, London W8.

NATIONAL ASSOCIATION OF CITIZENS' ADVICE BUREAUX CLASSIFICATION SCHEME

The National Association of Citizens' Advice Bureaux is the association which co-ordinates and provides training and information to the 900 or so independent Citizens' Advice Bureaux that exist throughout the country. One of the key services that NACAB provides to the individual bureaux is the detailed information pack which is produced fortnightly and contains an enormous quantity of pamphlets, government publications and detailed in-house information sheets on the problems that CAB clients will require assistance with.

This information pack is classified within the NACAB information department using a very broad 16-category classification scheme. The example given (figure 19) shows that the classification scheme breaks up social welfare problems into broad areas such as transport and communications, consumer, family and so on. Within each of the broad categories there are further, more detailed subdivisions which ensure that there is some sort of overall structure to the arrangements of the information files within CAB. However, the classification is extremely broad with no ability to synthesize concepts to give more detailed arrangements or further breakdown. As we have seen in the earlier section on physical arrangement and broad subject ordering this approach does mean that information workers and advice givers are forced to browse through sections of the file to ensure that they can find all the relevant information. This browsing process is an important part of information work, and ensures that there is a high level of recall from the retrieval system. Nonetheless, as files get larger and the sophistication of information becomes more complex a broad classification of this sort becomes difficult to use.

Particular difficulties result when advice agencies and bureaux start to integrate their locally-indexed information into the more general files. The level of specificity required for much of this local information defeats a general classification scheme of the sort that NACAB use at present. More and more information is placed in

```
9              SOCIAL SECURITY


9.1            Appeals
9.1.0
9.1.1          National Insurance Appeals
9.1.2          Medical Appeals
9.1.3          Supplementary Benefit Appeals
9.1.4          Representation

9.2            Benefits
9.2.0          General
9.2.1
9.2.2          Attendance Allowance
9.2.3          Death Grant
9.2.4
9.2.5
9.2.6          Earnings Related Benefit
9.2.7          Child Benefit
9.2.8
9.2.9.         Guardians Allowance
9.2.10         Child's Special Allowance
9.2.11
9.2.12         Retirement Pension
9.2.13         Sickness and Invalidity Benefit
9.2.14         Supplementary Benefit
9.2.15         Unemployment Benefit
9.2.16         War Pension
9.2.17         Other Payments
9.2.18         Widows Benefits
9.2.19         Industrial Death Benefit
9.2.20         Industrial Diseases
9.2.21         Industrial Injuries
9.2.22         Non-Contributory Benefits for Chronically Sick
9.2.23         Family Income Supplement
9.2.24
9.2.25         Maternity Benefit

9.3            Contributions
9.3.0
9.3.1          Payment
9.3.2
9.3.3          Refunds

9.4            Administration
9.4.0          General
9.4.1          Advisory Committees
9.4.2          Reciprocal Agreements
```

Reproduced with the permission of the National Association of Citizens' Advice Bureaux.

19 Part of the Social security category (9) from the old NACAB classification scheme

broad categories, with the resulting costs of time and effort in retrieving it.

It was because of these problems that NACAB set up in 1981 a classification research project to design and test a fully faceted classification scheme in the area of social welfare. It was envisaged from the start that this classification scheme would be used for both information and case-recording within information and advice centres, and that it would be designed as both a detailed faceted classification scheme and a thesaurus.

The bulk of the initial research work involved analysing client problems using detailed anonymous case-sheets in 90 Citizens' Advice Bureaux and a similar number of other advice agencies across the country. These case-sheets were completed for a month in each centre, and the information on problems was then gathered together. The research team was able to identify the likelihood of particular problems co-occurring with other problems. Three-way correlation, enabled an analysis of how each problem co-occurred with two other problems throughout the entire range of bureaux and advice centres. These raw data are obviously a powerful tool in allowing a classification scheme to match known client needs. The regularity of problems such as unemployment and housing co-occurring with debt and marital breakdown allows decisions on facets and orders of terms within facets to be resolved.

Schedules and facets

The resulting classification scheme is at an embryonic pilot stage, and should be in Citizens' Advice Bureaux by 1986. The whole approach of the classification scheme is geared up towards client problems, and there is an attempt to separate out those problems that are one-off or crisis problems such as birth, death or marriage from the more general on-going problems such as poverty and ill-health. There are also facets for people or persons and agencies of relief. The resulting facet structure is identified in figure 20.

The resulting classification scheme will be similar to that of Bliss in that it will have an inverted schedule, with the general facets coming first followed by the more specific ones, and number building will be retroactive, with the numbers from the most important facets at the end of the schedule being cited first followed by the more general ones coming early on in the schedules.

This classification scheme is a specialist subject-oriented retrieval

```
531 . . SOCIAL ISSUES & PROBLEMS & POLICIES
                    (including functions or
                    parts of the state)
551 . . . Parliament
576 . . . International relations
582 . . . War & peace
598 . . . Adminstration of justice
642 . . . Local government
672 . . . Energy policy
679 . . . Nationalisation & privatisation
681 . . . Cuts
700 . . . Environmental issues
711 . . . . Pollution & public health
713 . . . . Nuclear energy & waste & arms

715 . . PERSONAL ISSUES & PROBLEMS
719 . . . Assisting agencies
788 . . . Administration
790 . . . . . Funding
796 . . . . Techniques of helping people
829 . . . Techniques used by people to help
                    themselves
830 . . . . Legal action
955 . . . Types of people
1012. . . . Children & young people
                    *See also: 1300
1054. . . . Elderly people
1073. . . . Gay people
1082. . . . Women
1092. . . . Immigrants
                    *See also: 2420
1102. . . . Ethnic groups
1112. . . . Race & race relations
1181. . . . Unemployed & unemployment
                    *See also: 1716
1199. . . Types of personal problems & issues
1216. . . . Units of interaction
1300. . . . . Caring units
1344. . . . . . Families
1352. . . . . . . One parent families
1382. . . . . . Marital problmes
1396. . . . . . Family planning
                    *See also: 3289
1425. . . . . . . Pregnancy
1426. . . . . . . Birth
1427. . . . . . . Adoption
1436. . . . . . Children in care
1455. . . . . . Battered women
```

20 Part of a research draft of the new NACAB classification scheme

language, which means that the level of specificity given in the schedules will be high. When allied with the synthetic number-building qualities of a faceted classification scheme this will result in a very specific retrieval language with a high level of precision in retrieval. The cost will, of course, be long notation and an apparent complexity of number building for both the classifier and the searcher. However, this classification scheme will be primarily an in-house one, with a large amount of classification taking place at source within the NACAB information department. Thus, the early years of training and management development for the classifying process can be centralized. Once the classification scheme is adopted by individual bureaux and agencies they will slowly be able to identify the full advantages of such a detailed classification scheme.

All faceted classification schemes can, of course, be used at a number of different levels. A full analysis of items resulting in a multi-faceted synthesized classmark can take place for the key parts of a collection, possibly done centrally. An information unit can, however, decide to analyse items to a more limited level, perhaps using the initial facet structure, or possibly a combination of two facets only. Such an approach for local ephemeral information would result in a high-recall system that stimulates browsing and therefore a detailed knowledge of the collection. For much current awareness material such a broad-based browsing approach for the few weeks of relevance may be far more cost-effective than time spent on detailed classification. This multiple-level approach to faceted classification schemes also means that information units can receive pre-classified material but still decide to make use only of the initial facets cited in each classmark. The increased time spent in searching may be matched by the reduced time spent in filing.

The classification research project of National Association of Citizens' Advice Bureaux was funded for a two-year period by the British Library, and is based in the NACAB headquarters in Pentonville Road. The pilot schedules will be tested during the spring and summer of 1986, and further information will be available from NACAB, 115–123 Pentonville Road, London N1.

5 Alphabetical subject approaches

ALPHABETICAL SUBJECT HEADINGS

Alphabetical subject headings have always had a major role to play in many information-retrieval systems. Just as classification schemes seem to offer a very neat and creative way of showing searchers the links and relationships that exist between subjects so alphabetical subject headings seem to offer an approach based on the very words and phrases that searchers use in everyday speech. There seems to be an innate simplicity about designing a retrieval system that allows searchers to think of the words that describe the problems they are interested in and then look them up to find information that answers the particular problem. It is from this belief that the alphabetical subject approach develops.

One problem immediately emerges, which is that it is not possible to use alphabetical subject headings for the physical arrangement of books and other major documents. This is due to the problem of writing the subject heading on the item itself as much as the universal order that might result on the shelf. It is because of this that the majority of book-based libraries rely on classification schemes for their physical stock arrangement. They then have the choice between alphabetical or classified approaches for their supporting indexes and catalogues. This factor may be less relevant when dealing with files of information which could conceivably be arranged using alphabetical subject headings, although it would become quite difficult to file and search as the system became large.

Thus we have already moved from the possibility of a user thinking of a subject word that is used in everyday speech, consulting it in the system and finding the actual data or information at that word. The user must consult the word in an index or catalogue, be given a classmark or some other piece of code and then move to the shelves or the filing cabinet to find the actual information. However, this process is no more difficult than that faced by the user in a classified approach, who has to consult the subject index to translate the word in everyday speech into the classmark in the notation of the classification scheme so that the shelves or the classified catalogue can be searched.

Having accepted the initial drawback of the alphabetical subject approach in physically arranging material in retrieval systems, there are obviously some other advantages and disadvantages. The initial advantage of using a retrieval language that matches the terms used by the searcher in everyday occurrence is marred by the fact that it is often very difficult to get agreement on what words actually mean. Terms such as **unemployment benefit, the dole, supplementary benefit,** and **welfare benefits** all have shades of overlapping meaning depending very often on who is using them. We shall need to design a system where both the searcher and the indexer can agree on what all the various terms mean.

Similarly, there is a problem concerning relationships, **supplementary benefit, housing benefit** and **unemployment benefit** are all separate concepts that are strongly related to each other. The alphabetical arrangement of the retrieval system will scatter items on these three concepts at different places in the file. We shall need to make sure that there is a structure in the catalogue or index to ensure that searchers can be guided from one particular access point to another so that they can widen their search and pick up a whole range of related material.

In the classified approach, of course, this problem is solved by ensuring that all such related material is filed very close together under classmarks that file one after another. The example of an alphabetical subject approach given from the *Cumulative Book Index* (see figure 21) shows how searchers are led from one subject heading such as **Brain** to others such as **Memory**, through the use of *see also* references. Thus the user can enter the system at a particular subject heading, find all the relevant items and then be led to a wider range of alternative subject headings under which there might be linked material.

At the same time those terms that mean the same thing, such as **unemployment benefit** and **the dole** are linked together through *see* references which refer the searcher from the term not used to the one that it has been decided to use. Thus an entry would read **dole** *see* **unemployment benefit**. At **unemployment benefit** would be all the

21 A page from the *Cumulative Book Index*

information relating to that concept, followed by *see also* references leading across to items such as **housing benefit** and **supplementary benefit**. This type of approach is called a syndetic structure.

One of the particular advantages of such an alphabetical subject approach, with all the *see* and *see also* references interfiled with various entries carrying different subject headings, is that authors and titles can also be interfiled to form an extremely large single sequence of all approaches and access points to the complete collection. Such a catalogue is called a dictionary catalogue and has a long history in many libraries in the United States. The *Cumulative Book Index* is an excellent example of such a dictionary catalogue, and the *British Humanities Index* is a fine example of a subject arrangement using alphabetical headings (see figure 22).

In order to make use of alphabetical subject headings it is important that we have a tool or authority file that allows us to agree on:

a) the particular terms that we would allow as access points in the system;
b) the synonyms that will become *see* references in the system;
c) the subject relationships that we will link together through *see also* references in the system.

A number of general subject-headings lists that fulfil this role are used in academic and public libraries, and there are many specialist lists in different subject fields. Two general subject-headings lists that exist are *The Library of Congress list of subject headings* and *Sears list of subject headings*. The former was produced for the Library of Congress in the United States and the latter was produced for a range of medium-sized American public libraries.

Most subject headings lists have grown in an ad hoc fashion over the years as indexers have inserted words or phrases that seem to be reasonable subject headings, and then linked them to their synonyms using *see* references, and to their related concepts through *see also* references. The result is that these tools tend to be rather a mish-mash of different types of subject heading with very little consistency. Nonetheless they reflect the sort of ad hoc intuitive approach that many small information units without sufficient time or staff might be adopting in order to satisfy their very varying user needs.

Social Networks
Perceived humor and social network patterns in a sample of task-oriented groups: a reexamination of prior research. W. Jack Duncan. Human Relations, 37 (Nov 84) p.895-907. refs.

Social Psychology
William McDougall in the history of social psychology. Floyd Rudmin. Brit. J. of Social Psychology, 24 (Feb 85) p.75-6. refs.

Social Psychology
Related Headings:
Group Psychology
Relationships, Interpersonal

Social Research *see* Sociology: Research

Social Sciences
Related Headings:
Sociology

Social Sciences: Philosophy
Social science, critical theory and history. Robert J. Tristram. Political Science, 36 (Dec 84) p.162-73. refs.

Social Security
Related Headings:
National Insurance
Sickness Benefits
Supplementary Benefits
Unemployment Benefits

Social Security: Great Britain
Battle royal of the welfare cuts. Nicholas Timmins. Times, (8 Feb 85) p.16. ports.
Britain's welfare future: tinkering with Beveridge. Economist, 294 (23 Feb 85) p.21+ (4 pages). il.
The concealed benefits of Mr Norman Fowler. David Hencke. Guardian, (17 Jan 85) p.17.
The determinants of attitudes towards social security recipients. Adrian Furnham. Brit. J. of Social Psychology, 24 (Feb 85) p.19-27. refs.
Integration — but not behind closed doors. [Tax and social security systems]. Nicholas Timmins. Times, (22 Mar 85) p.16.
Let them eat humble pie. Gordon Brown. New Statesman, (8 Feb 85) p.13-15. port.
Making allowances for jobs. Sarah Hogg. Times, (19 Feb 85) p.12.
Reforming the social security system: a critique of the IFS proposals. Stephen Jenkins. Political Q., 56 (Jan/Mar 85) p.33-46. refs.
Rough justice. Tony Lynes. New Society, 71 (21 Feb 85) p.301-2. il.
A way out of the poverty trap. Michael Meacher. Times, (18 Mar 85) p.12.

Social Security: Great Britain
Related Headings:
Homeless: Great Britain
National Insurance: Great Britain
Sickness Benefits: Great Britain
Supplementary Benefits: Great Britain

22 An extract from *British Humanities Index*

SEARS LIST OF SUBJECT HEADINGS

This vocabulary, designed for use in medium-sized public libraries, contains about 10,000 entry terms, of which about 5,000 are allowed as preferred subject headings. Each heading that is used as an access point is given in bold type, such as **Social problems** and each term is then followed by three lists of the other terms in the system that are in some way related. As the example (figure 23) shows, each term is followed by a list headed *see also* which indicates the more specific terms that exist within the system and which the indexer might prefer to the one initially consulted. Following that there are two lists, one preceded by a single *x* which indicates that these are words which are synonyms to the one consulted and which should not be used, but be given *see* references leading from the terms following the *x* to the heading which has been chosen.

Social problems
  See also

Charities	**Migrant labor**
Child labor	**Old age pensions**
Community centers	**Prostitution**
Cost and standard	**Public health**
of living	**Race problems**
Crime and criminals	**Social ethics**
Discrimination	**Social surveys**
Divorce	**Suicide**
Eugenics	**Tenement houses**
Housing	**Unemployed**
Immigration and	**Woman—Employ-**
emigration	**ment**
Juvenile delin-	**Woman—Social and**
quency	**moral questions**
Liquor problem	

    x Reform, Social; Social reform; Social welfare
    xx Civilization; Social conditions; Social ethics; Sociology

Social problems and the church. *See* **Church and social problems**

Social problems in education. *See* **Educational sociology**

23 An entry from *Sears list of subject headings*

There then follows a brief list preceded by a *xx* which means that these are terms which are related to the one chosen and that *see also* references should be given from these terms to the heading chosen.

Thus we can see that the tool is simple to use; an indexer identifies the term that appears to be reasonable as a subject heading for the document and looks it up in the headings list. If it is in bold type and the list of more specific terms given in the *see also* column does not suggest any better heading then it is the correct term to use. That term could go on top of a 5 × 3 card for the particular item, and *see* references are made from the terms in the list preceded by the *x* and *see also* references are made from the terms preceded by the *xx*. Thus for a book on social problems we would enter it under the subject heading **social problems** and make references as follows:

> Reform, social *see* Social problems
> Social reform *see* Social problems
> Social welfare *see* Social problems
> Social conditions *see also* Social problems
> Social ethics *see also* Social problems
> Sociology *see also* Social problems

These references are made when this first item is added in this subject area, and they then stand for all other items added.

PROBLEMS IN THE ALPHABETICAL SUBJECT APPROACH

Problems arise when subject headings are needed that consist of more than a single term. Few retrieval systems can survive using simply single terms and most need to be able to specify elements such as **library administration** or **housing benefits for the elderly**. Sears indicates that such compound terms are allowed, but unfortunately is extremely inconsistent in showing the order in which such terms should be placed. Thus **Library administration** is allowed but so is **Acquisitions (libraries)**. Similarly **Literature and science** is allowed but so also is **Religion and literature**. It is this sort of inconsistency which shows the very ad hoc growth in Sears and similar traditional subject headings lists. For both the searcher and the indexer this inconsistency is irritating.

This difficulty over the order in which terms should go when there are more than one is exactly the same problem as we had in the faceted classification schemes when we were discussing the order in which the various concepts from different facets should be placed when synthesizing the classmark. Citation order, as it was called in the chapters on classification theory, is primarily the problem of the order in which we put concepts in a string of index terms or a classmark. The difficulties over identifying a particular citation order in traditional lists such as Sears or Library of Congress resulted in a far more theoretical approach to the whole business of producing alphabetical subject headings.

Citation orders

Sears enumerated very simple compound subjects in an ad hoc and inconsistent way. In terms of development the headings produced are very similar to some of the classmarks found in the traditional classification schemes such as Dewey. A subject heading should be co-extensive with the subject content of a document and should therefore be a string of terms that precisely describes that document. In order to produce that string of terms we need a citation order that allows both the indexer and the searcher to work out how to access the system. Once the citation order has been agreed upon the various index terms can be synthesized together from a simple list of single terms. This approach is shown in a tool such as the *Current Technology Index* (see figure 24) in which the citation order adopted is based on the type of concepts involved. The preferred order is: thing, part, material, action, property. The idea of the citation order, or significance formula as it was originally called, is that detailed co-extensive subject headings can be produced for all documents in the same way as the classmarks are synthesized in a faceted classification scheme. Entries such as:

BONES
  Joints, artificial: Polythene, High density:
  Testing

are formalized strings that have moved away from normal language and use citation orders that searchers can work out in a logical fashion before the search is started. In *CTI* the terms in the string are even synthesized using punctuation which shows particular relationships. Once the citation order and vocabulary or thesaurus have produced the detailed subject string for the document, the user must be led from those parts of the subject heading which are not the lead term or entry point to the place where all the information can be found. This requires a number of references which allow any

BOILING, Nucleate
See
Water : Boiling, Nucleate
BOILING HELIUM
See
Helium, Boiling
BOMB DAMAGED HOTELS
See
Hotels, Bomb damaged
BOMBS
See
Aircraft, Military : Bombs
BONDED HOLLOW GLASS SPHERES
See
Glass spheres, Hollow, Bonded
BONDED LAPPED JOINTS
See
Aircraft : Structures : Aluminium—Magnesium—
Zinc, Clad : Iron : Joints, Lapped, Bonded

BONE, Substitute

Calcium phosphate, Tribasic, Sintered :
Biodegradation
Interaction of biodegradable β-whitlockite
ceramics with bone tissue: an in vivo study.
C.P.A.T. Klein, K. de Groot, A.A. Driessen &
H.B.M. van der Lubbe. *Biomaterials*, 6 (May 85)
p.189-92

BONES

Joints, Artificial : Polythene, High density :
Testing
Comparison of RCH 1000 and Hi-Fax 1900 ultra-
high molecular weight polyethylenes. [Hoechst.
RCH 1000] [Hercules Hifax 1900] B.
Weightman & D. Light. *Biomaterials*, 6 (May
85) p.177-83

BOOSTERS
See
Ships : Diesel engines, Turbocompound :
Turbochargers : Boosters
BOOTHS
See
Paint : Spraying : Booths
BOREHOLES
See
Ground water : Boreholes
BORING
See
District heating : Tunnels : Boring
Railways : Tunnels : Boring
Railways, Underground : Tunnels : Boring
Tunnels : Boring
Water : Supplies : Inter-river transfer : Tunnels :
Boring
BORON
See
Rock : Silicates : Determination of boron

BORON NITRIDE, Cubic

Machining
'Ultrahards' for turning, milling. [De Beers:
Amborite] A. Notter. *Machinery Prod. Engng.*,
143 (1 May 85) p.47-8

BORON—PHOSPHORUS—IRON—CHROMIUM—
NICKEL
See
Iron—Chromium—Nickel—Boron—Phosphorus
BOROSILICATE GLASS
See
Glass, Borosilicate
BOTTLES
See
Drinks, Soft : Bottles
BOUNDARY LAYER
See
Aerofoils, Biconvex : Flow, Transonic : Boundary
layer

BOUNDARY LAYER, Blasius

Analysis : Orr—Sommerfeld equation :
Solution
Uniformly valid solution of the Orr-Sommerfeld
equation by a modified Heisenberg method. S.
Tsuge & H. Sakai. *J. Fluid Mech.*, 153 (Apr 85)
p.167-83

BOUNDARY LAYER, Laminar
See
Aircraft : Wings, Swept : Leading edges :
Boundary layer, Turbulent : Transition from
laminar
BOUNDARY LAYER, Turbulent
See
Aircraft : Wings, Swept : Leading edges :
Boundary layer, Turbulent
Airflow : Boundary layer, Turbulent
BOX GIRDER BRIDGES
See
Bridges, Box girder

BOXES

Manual handling : Wrist deviation
Experiments on wrist deviation in manual
materials handling. C.G. Drury, K. Begbie, C.
Ulate & J.M. Deeb. *Ergonomics*, 28 (Mar 85)
p.577-89

BRAKES
See
Trucks : Brakes
BRANCHED FATTY ACIDS
See
Fatty acids, Branched

BREAD

Additives : Soya products
Progress with the traditional. L. Meyer. *Fd. Flavs.
Ingredients Process. Packag.*, 7 (May 85) p.59-
60

BREAKDOWN
See
Cables, Electric, Superconducting : Insulating
materials : Helium, Liquid : Breakdown

BRICKS

Bricks' proud heritage. J. Hayes. *Master Bldr.*, 30
(Jun 85) p.30+

BRIDGES

Bascule : Construction
Big lift technology beat the elements. [Breydon
Bridge, Great Yarmouth] *Highways*, 53 (Mar
85) p.34-5
Bascule : History
Tower Bridge. L.W. Groome, W.I. Halse, E.M.
Longton & D.L. Stephens. *Struct. Engr.*, 63A
(Feb 85) p.39-44
Box girder : Concrete, Post-tensioned
Design of Kylesku Bridge. J. Nissen, K. Falbe-
Hansen & H.S. Stears. *Struct. Engr.*, 63A (Mar
85) p.69-76

BRIQUETTING
See
Furnaces, Blast : Coal : Briquetting
BRITISH COLUMBIA
See
Fluorspar : Deposits : Quesnel Lake

BRITTLE MATERIALS

Bending : Stress—Strain relationships
Estimating damage laws from bend-test data.
A.R. Rosenfield, D.K. Shetty & W.H.
Duckworth. *J. Mater. Sci.*, 20 (Mar 85) p.935-
40

BRONZE
Related headings
Sodium tungsten bronze
BROWN COAL
See
Coal, Brown
BROWN COAL DERIVED ACTIVATED CARBON
See
Carbon, Activated, Brown coal derived
BUBBLES
See
Water : Bubbles
BUCKLING
See
Columns, Elastic : Buckling
Cylinders, Ring stiffened : Buckling
Plates, Rectangular, Elastic : Laminates : Buckling

BUFFERED SODIUM SULPHATE SOLUTIONS
See
Steel, Mild : Pitting : Sodium sulphate solutions,
Buffered

BUILDING

See also
Glass spheres, Hollow, Bonded : Aluminium
phosphate : Building materials
Stone : Building materials
Wood : Building materials
Related headings
Air conditioning
Architecture
Buildings
Ceilings
Doors
Floors
Rooms
Structures
Ventilation
Windows
Contracts
Beware! Nomination in progress. R. Robinson.
Building, 248 (19 Apr 85) p.30-1
Education, Management
Training for a new age. J. Bale. *Building*, 248 (24
May 85) p.38-9
Industry : North East England
Private developers are still confident in region's
future. *Contract J.*, 325 (30 May 85) p.20-1
Microcomputers
Maximising the micro. M. Dyer. *Archit. Surv.*, 60
(Apr/May 85) p.9-11
Regulations : Great Britain
Building Regulations—the way forward. G.
Young. *Archit. Surv.*, 59 (Dec 84/Jan 85)
p.11+
Research : Computers : Programs, Expert
system
Expert systems. M.R. Shaw. *Bldg. Serv.*, 7 (May
85) p.71
Safety
Industry strives to halt safety slide. S.
McCormack. *New Civ. Engr.* (16 May 85)
p.20+
Sites : Personnel : Helmets, Safety
Research to improve safety helmets.
[Loughborough University of Technology.
Institute for Consumer Ergonomics] T.D.
Proctor & E.M. Hickling. *Wk. Study*, 34 (Apr
85) p.37-40

BUILDING BLOCKS, Storage unit
See
Architecture : Design, Computer aided : Models :
Building blocks, Storage unit

BUILDINGS

Related headings
Art galleries
Commercial buildings
Conference buildings
Educational buildings
Industrial buildings
Medical buildings
Religious buildings
Residential buildings
Sports buildings
Coatings, Flame resistant
Flame retardant coatings. J. Stenton. *Archit.
Surv.*, 59 (Dec 84/Jan 85) p.14-15
Concrete : Repair
Concrete maintenance in building: cause and
effect. G. Atkinson. *Building*, 248 (19 Apr 85)
p.46-7
Concrete : Repair : Contractors
Concrete maintenance in building: the solution. B.
Long. *Building*, 248 (19 Apr 85) p.49-50
Energy utilisation : Town planning : Milton
Keynes
Innovation takes root in new city's £100m park
venture. [Milton Keynes Energy Park] J.
Walker. *Surveyor*, 165 (16 May 85) p.9-11
Milton Keynes Energy Park. *Energy Dig.*, 14 no.2
(1985) p.3-5
Engineering services : Control systems,
Computerised
Systems management. W. Watson. *Plant Engr.*,
29 (Mar/Apr 85) p.21-4

24 A page from *Current Technology Index*

term in the subject heading string to be accessed by different users and so be led eventually to that term which is the lead term of the correct subject heading string. Thus

BUILDING BLOCKS, Storage unit
  See
  Architecture: Design, Computer-aided: Models:
    Building blocks, Storage unit

This large number of references can rather mar the use of such an alphabetical subject tool.

This structured approach to producing alphabetical subject headings means that they can now be as precise as a faceted classification scheme in describing exactly the subject content of a particular item, and at the same time allow the use of normal language rather than a coding or notation. This means that the tool used to provide the vocabulary for the information-retrieval system becomes a thesaurus rather than a traditional subject-headings list. The essential difference is that a thesaurus shows single terms, which can then be synthesized together using the citation order to produce co-extensive index strings or left as single terms for postcoordinate searching. A subject-headings list was not designed for this sort of approach, and merely gives an ad hoc collection of some synthesized compounds such as **Science and religion** and rarely allows the indexer to produce subject headings which precisely and co-extensively describe the content of a document. In this respect they are very similar to the traditional enumerative classification schemes discussed elsewhere.

A particularly interesting example of an information-retrieval system using a thesaurus, but linked with a formal citation order is that produced by the Library Board of Western Australia.

WESTERN AUSTRALIA SUBJECT-HEADINGS LIST

This thesaurus was produced for a community information service in 1983 and is a thesaurus or subject-headings list designed so that the indexer can synthesize terms together using a particular citation order. The citation order is made very clear in the thesaurus and is based on a process of facet analysis.

Terms are arranged alphabetically in the thesaurus and those terms that are allowed as access points are entered in capitals and underlined; for example *EDUCATIONAL ASSESSMENT* is a used term and is entered as follows

(1) <u>EDUCATIONAL ASSESSMENT</u>

> Diagnostic services aimed at detecting
> causes of learning difficulty
> UF   Assessment, Educational
> RT   <u>SPECIFIC LEARNING DIFFICULTIES</u>
>
> <u>SUPPLEMENTARY TUTORING</u>
>
> <u>VOCATIONAL GUIDANCE</u>

The UF stands for 'use for' and indicates that **Assessment, educational** is a non-preferred inversion of the used term. The RT or 'related terms' indicates those terms that are related but appear elsewhere in the thesaurus because of the alphabetical arrangement. Figure 25 gives a whole page from the thesaurus, and it can be seen that although there are certain compound terms most of the access points are simple concepts.

An item is indexed by lifting out the terms from the thesaurus that are relevant and then combining them in a string following the preferred citation order. This preferred citation order is based on the five main groups into which all terms have been assigned. Each of these groups is given a number from one to five, and it is that number which is alongside each term in the thesaurus. The five groups are:

1 Service term
2 Agent term
3 Client term
4 Common modifier
5 Locality term

Thus we have three major facets of Services, Agents and Clients, and a group of common modifiers that is a general facet covering concepts such as clubs, evaluation, research, or volunteers. There are only 15 terms that are common modifiers and they can only be added to another term; in other words they are synthetic devices that increase specificity but cannot stand on their own. The final facet is locality terms which are place terms which do not appear in

Damages
Use COMPENSATION

(1) DANCING
NT BALLET
    FOLK DANCING
    OLD-TIME DANCING

(3) DANISH
UF Scandinavian

(1) DARTS

(1) DAY CARE
UF After school care
RT ADOPTION
    EMERGENCY CARE
    FOSTER FAMILY CARE
    PRE-SCHOOLS

Day Care, Family
Use FAMILY DAY CARE

(1) DAY CARE (FULL)
At least 35 hours per week
UF Full day care
    Long day care
RT DAY CARE (PART)
    FAMILY DAY CARE
    HOLIDAY CARE
    OUTSIDE SCHOOL HOURS CARE

(1) DAY CARE (PART)
Less than 35 hours per week
includes part & occasional care.
UF Occasional care
RT DAY CARE (FULL)
    FAMILY DAY CARE
    HOLIDAY CARE
    OUTSIDE SCHOOL HOURS CARE

(1) DEAD ANIMAL COLLECTION
UF Collecting dead animals
RT STREET CLEANING
    WASTE DISPOSAL

(3) DEAF
UF Hearing impairment
    Lipreading
RT AUDIOLOGY

Dealers, motor cars
Use MOTOR-CAR DEALERS

(1) DEATH AND DYING COUNSELLING
UF Bereavement support
    Grief support

Death duties
Use PROBATE

(1) DEATHS/LICENSING & REGULATIONS
UF Death certificates

(1) DEBATING

Debt management
Use FINANCIAL COUNSELLING

(1) DECENTRALISATION
RT RESETTLEMENT
    TOURISM

Decorating, interiors
Use INTERIOR DECORATING

Deed Poll
Use CHANGE OF NAME/LICENSING
    & REGULATION

(1) DE FACTO RELATIONSHIPS

Defamation
Use LEGAL SERVICE

Defense, civil
Use CIVIL DEFENSE

(3) DELINQUENTS
UF Juvenile offenders

(1) DEMOLITIONS

(1) DENTAL SERVICES
UF Oral Health
RT DENTISTS

(2) DENTISTS
RT DENTAL SERVICES

Derelicts
Use DESTITUTE

Deserted fathers
Use SINGLE PARENT FAMILIES

(3) DESERTED HUSBANDS
UF Husband, deserted
RT SINGLE PARENT FAMILIES

Deserted mothers
Use SINGLE PARENT FAMILIES

(3) DESERTED WIVES
UF Wives, deserted
RT SINGLE PARENT FAMILIES

25 A page from the *Western Australia subject headings list*

the thesaurus itself but can be added as the last term in a compound string.

These five facets must be joined together in the order of their numbers; thus a term prefixed in the thesaurus by a (1) must always come before terms prefixed by (2), (3), (4) or (5). Thus we have a citation order of service-agent-client and that citation order is shown in the body of the thesaurus by the numbers prefixing each of the preferred terms.

The thesaurus is therefore giving both the vocabulary and the citation order in a way that allows indexing to be specific and co-extensive with the subject content of each item and at the same time enables it to be done with the minimum of effort and time. Because the citation order has to be rigorously adhered to there is no possibility of inconsistencies occurring in strings of compound terms.

The service terms in the thesaurus are those that come first in the citation order and they describe the activities provided by organizations to assist or benefit the local community. The agent terms are those services which deal with the licensing and regulation of, or complaints about, people who provide particular services, for example dentists, landlords, etc. The third group or facet are clients who are the target or recipients of a particular service and they will include specific groups such as Italians or Aborigines or particular groups of disadvantaged people such as the blind. These three key facets are synthesized together using an oblique stroke resulting in strings such as **Education/Blind**. On to this can be added a common modifier such as **Advocacy group** to produce a string such as **Education/Blind/Advocacy groups**.

In order that users can always find information irrespective of the particular access point they enter the system under, it is suggested that a reference structure is built into the retrieval system as was outlined earlier in the section on the alphabetical subject approach. Thus the entry **Education/Blind** will be on a 5 × 3 card containing full information about the relevant document. The entry **Blind, Education** is a reference which reads **Blind, Education use EDUCATION / BLIND**. This system of multiple entry ensures that for each string of index terms there is one entry containing the full information and a series of back-up references leading from the other terms to the preferred entry term. This of course increases the size of the retrieval system but does ensure that users generally obtain the relevant information in the end. It is hoped, of course, that the use of a rigorous citation order identified in the thesaurus will be grasped by the searchers who will be able to use the thesaurus to formulate their search strategies. The prefixing of each entry term with the number for the citation order means that, providing they consult the thesaurus, every searcher will be able to formulate a search strategy by recognizing that **Blind** is given the number (3) and therefore will normally come after service or agent term. This then forces the searcher to identify the service or agent terms that might be relevant to the particular enquiry and structure the search accordingly. The reference structure in the main retrieval system is therefore a back-up device for those who are unable to formulate a search strategy from the thesaurus itself.

PRODUCING A THESAURUS

A thesaurus is obviously a key tool in the subject analysis, indexing and retrieval of information in many units. Classification schemes are valuable in allowing certain sorts of searches, and structuring information in a way that shows relationships and stimulates new links whilst at the same time being free from the problems of using real words, but the problems and difficulties of identifying such relationships and structuring them through the hierarchical, two-dimensional system of a classification scheme may be difficult or even impossible. A thesaurus is a retrieval vocabulary which can be used for both indexing and searching in a number of different systems, and is therefore a tool which a number of information units will be keen to produce themselves.

There are a number of texts and agencies that can assist in thesaurus construction. The step-by-step guide produced by Elizabeth Orna *Build yourself a thesaurus* is fairly essential as is Aitchison and Gilchrist's *Thesaurus construction, a practical manual*. The section on the Western Australia subject-headings list gave a good example of what a thesaurus looks like and how it can be used. The production of such a tool is time-consuming but worth while if no alternative is available. The task of shoe-horning a half-relevant vocabulary into an information unit can be more irritating and time-consuming than sitting down and producing a relevant one from scratch. This is particularly true of areas with disciplinary overlap such as community information. If a thesaurus is to be produced it is best to do it well – as once the vocabulary has been adopted in the information unit it is expensive and time-consuming to make major changes. The production of a thesaurus is a useful way of analysing the information materials within a unit, the information needs of users and the structure of the subject discipline. For many new information units the process of making a thesaurus is often a valuable starting-point for the development of the whole unit.

Producing a thesaurus consists of assembling terms and indicating the relationships between those terms. The process normally involves entering the terms on slips as they are identified, and then showing the broader, narrower and related links as each new term is added to the list. New terms will always be emerging and a thesaurus is never finally completed, but obviously a decision needs to be made on when the list can be typed out or printed for use as a working tool. Experience in thesaurus construction in such fields as management, with the British Institute of Management thesaurus, suggests that there is rapid growth in the number of new terms in the early part of thesaurus construction but that this gradually tails off so that a stage is reached when the new literature coming into the information unit generates only a very small number of new terms. It is at this stage that a thesaurus can be regarded as a working document rather than still in production. Alternatively, of course, a decision might have been made to use a very limited thesaurus with a small number of vocabulary terms in order to ensure a high level of recall and a relatively simple indexing process.

Literature within the unit is obviously the starting-point for term assembly, and the first terms will be acquired from titles, contents pages and the texts of items within the unit. As terms are assembled from the literature, decisions will need to be made on forms of name, whether single or plural, as well as policy decisions on the level of specificity to be allowed within the system. Thus a decision on the inclusion of, for example, libraries, librarians and librarianship all as separate index terms is effectively a decision on the level of specificity and therefore the level of precision within the retrieval system that the user will meet at the searching stage. As we saw in the theoretical section the greater the number of terms, the greater the specificity and therefore the greater the precision. Both Orna and Aitchison and Gilchrist give examples of the decision-making process for some of these issues, but the key decisions can be taken only by the persons producing the thesaurus for their own users.

As terms are assembled from the literature within the information unit other sources will need to be consulted. The other sources are of

Social Security
  TX1801
  UF Old Age and Survivor's Insurance
  BT Social Insurance
  NT Medicare
  RT Aged Persons (65 +)
    Aid to Families with Dependent Children
    Disability Insurance
    Eligibility Requirements
    Income Maintenance Programs
    Pensions Funds
    Pension Plans
    Pensions
    Retirement

Social Service Agencies
  TX4008
  BT Social Services
    Social Welfare
  NT Settlement Houses
    Adoption Agencies
    Social Service Exchanges
    Social Welfare Organizations
    Social Work
    Social Workers
    Umbrella Organizations
    Voluntary Agencies
    Volunteer Workers

Social Service Exchanges
  XT2707
  SN *Refers to clearinghouses of social service associations organized to prevent duplication of services to the same client*
  BT Social Welfare Organizations
  RT Information and Referral Services
    Social Service Agencies

Social Services
  TX2200
  BT Social Welfare
  NT Disaster Services
    Family Services
    Juvenile Services
    Physical Therapy
    Poverty Programs
    Protective Services
    Senior Citizens Centers
    Social Service Agencies

Reproduced with the permission of the Baltimore region Institutional Studies Centre.

26 A page from the *Urban information Thesaurus* by D M Rosenberg

two main groups. Firstly, text and information items not within the unit and secondly individuals concerned with either the subject fields or the unit.

Information-bearing sources outside the unit will be such items as encyclopaedias, yearbooks and journals. Obviously, if this is a new

SMOKING   *Apr 1969*
CIJE 177   RIE 107
UF   Cigarette Smoking
BT   Behavior
RT   Cancer
     Drug Abuse
     Drug Use
     Health Education
     Physical Health
     Stimulants
     Tobacco

Snack Bars
USE   DINING FACILITIES

Snowskiing
USE   SKIING

SOCCER   *Dec 1975*
CIJE 10   RIE 13
BT   Athletics

Sociability
USE   INTERPERSONAL COMPETENCE

SOCIAL ACTION   *Nov 1969*
CIJE 453   RIE 372
UF   Political Reform
     Social Reform
NT   Community Action
RT   Action Research
     Activism
     Citizen Participation
     Dissent
     Humanitarianism
     Revolution
     Social Attitudes
     Social Change
     Social Responsibility

SOCIAL ADJUSTMENT   *Jul 1966*
CIJE 450   RIE 573
UF   Socially Maladjusted (1956 1980)
BT   Adjustment (To Environment)
     Social Behavior
RT   Alienation
     Conformity
     Interpersonal Competence
     Social Development
     Social Influences
     Social Isolation
     Social Problems

SOCIAL AGENCIES   *Jul 1966*
CIJE 100   RIE 146
SN   Nonprofit, voluntary, and/or tax-supported service organizations
NT   Welfare Agencies
BT   Agencies
RT   Agency Role
     Public Agencies
     Social Services
     Social Work
     Social Workers
     Voluntary Agencies

SOCIAL ATTITUDES   *Jul 1966*
CIJE 1,470   RIE 1,113
SN   Attitudes of individuals or groups with respect to social objects or phenomena such as persons, races, institutions, or traits
NT   Social Bias
BT   Attitudes
RT   Activism
     Alienation
     Community Attitudes
     Dissent
     Egocentrism
     Interpersonal Competence
     Justice
     Language Attitudes
     Political Attitudes
     Political Socialization
     Public Opinion
     Regional Attitudes

Social Action
Social Change
Social Characteristics
Social Development
Social Differences
Social Environment
Social Influences
Social Problems
Social Values

Social Awareness
USE   INTERPERSONAL COMPETENCE

SOCIAL BACKGROUND   *Jul 1966*
CIJE 74   RIE 111
NT   Social Experience
BT   Socioeconomic Background
RT   Social Class
     Social Influences

SOCIAL BEHAVIOR   *Dec 1970*
CIJE 656   RIE 608
SN   Behavior influenced or controlled by other persons or by organized society
UF   Social Norms ●
NT   Activism
     Antisocial Behavior
     Conformity
     Dissent
     Prosocial Behavior
     Social Adjustment
BT   Behavior
RT   Assertiveness
     Behavior Development
     Competition
     Cooperation
     Group Behavior
     Interaction Process Analysis
     Interpersonal Competence
     Psychological Patterns
     Social Influences
     Sociology
     Sociometric Techniques
     Stranger Reactions

SOCIAL BIAS   *Mar 1980*
CIJE 560   RIE 460
SN   Prejudicial attitudes toward particular groups, races, sexes, or religions, including the conscious or unconscious expression of these attitudes in writing, speaking, etc (note: do not confuse with various "discrimination" terms, which refer to the actions based on those attitudes)
UF   Discriminatory Attitudes (Social) (1966 1980)
NT   Ethnic Bias
     Racial Bias
     Sex Bias
BT   Bias
     Social Attitudes
RT   Cultural Differences
     Discriminatory Legislation
     Intergroup Relations
     Minority Groups
     Nature Nurture Controversy
     Negative Attitudes
     Religious Discrimination
     Social Discrimination

SOCIAL CHANGE   *Jul 1966*
CIJE 2,339   RIE 2,129
SN   Evolution or change at the societal, rather than individual, level, possibly involving the restructuring of political and/or economic relations (note: prior to mar80, the use of this term was not restricted by a scope note)
UF   Social Reconstruction
     Societal Change
BT   Change
RT   Change Agents
     Change Strategies
     Community Change
     Culture Lag

Economic Development
Futures (Of Society)
Political Influences
Political Socialization
Revolution
Social Action
Social Attitudes
Social History
Social Indicators
Social Influences
Social Integration
Social Problems
Social Values
Sociocultural Patterns

SOCIAL CHARACTERISTICS   *Jul 1966*
CIJE 127   RIE 247
SN   Criteria used to rate members of a social class
RT   Cultural Context
     Cultural Traits
     Individual Characteristics
     Interpersonal Competence
     Place Of Residence
     Regional Characteristics
     Social Attitudes
     Social Class
     Social Differences
     Social Environment
     Social Indicators
     Social Influences
     Social Values
     Sociology

SOCIAL CLASS   *Jul 1966*
CIJE 478   RIE 385
NT   Caste
     Lower Class
     Lower Middle Class
     Middle Class
     Upper Class
BT   Groups
RT   Income
     Quality Of Life
     Social Background
     Social Characteristics
     Social Dialects
     Social Differences
     Social Distribution
     Social Integration
     Social Status
     Social Stratification
     Social Structure
     Socioeconomic Status
     Status
     Subcultures

Social Class Differences
USE   SOCIAL DIFFERENCES

Social Class Integration
USE   SOCIAL INTEGRATION

Social Climate
USE   SOCIAL ENVIRONMENT

Social Competence
USE   INTERPERSONAL COMPETENCE

SOCIAL DEVELOPMENT   *Jul 1966*
CIJE 732   RIE 1,206
SN   Pattern or process of change exhibited by individuals resulting from their interaction with other individuals, social institutions, social customs, etc (note: do not confuse with "social change" -- prior to mar80, the use of this term was not restricted by a scope note)
BT   Individual Development
RT   Egocentrism
     Friendship
     Individualism
     Interpersonal Competence
     Mate Selection
     Personality Development
     Perspective Taking
     Social Adjustment

Social Attitudes
Social Differences
Social Environment
Social Experience
Social Influences
Socialization
Social Life

SOCIAL DIALECTS   *Jul 1966*
CIJE 138   RIE 232
SN   Special varieties within a language, defined by the social environment of its speakers
BT   Dialects
RT   Black Dialects
     Diglossia
     Language
     Language Role
     Linguistics
     Nonstandard Dialects
     Regional Dialects
     Social Class
     Standard Spoken Usage
     Urban Language

SOCIAL DIFFERENCES   *Jul 1966*
CIJE 345   RIE 409
UF   Social Class Differences
BT   Differences
RT   Cultural Differences
     Culture Conflict
     Individual Differences
     Intermarriage
     Racial Differences
     Rural Urban Differences
     Social Attitudes
     Social Characteristics
     Social Class
     Social Development
     Social Environment
     Social Integration
     Social Values

Social Disadvantagement (1966 1980)
USE   DISADVANTAGED

SOCIAL DISCRIMINATION   *Jul 1966*
CIJE 363   RIE 474
UF   Bigotry
     Discrimination (Social)
NT   Age Discrimination
     Educational Discrimination
     Ethnic Discrimination
     Housing Discrimination
     Racial Discrimination
     Religious Discrimination
     Reverse Discrimination
     Sex Discrimination
RT   Caste
     Civil Rights
     Civil Rights Legislation
     Discriminatory Legislation
     Equal Facilities
     Ghettos
     Intergroup Relations
     Minority Groups
     Segregationist Organizations
     Social Bias
     Social Integration
     Test Bias

SOCIAL DISTRIBUTION   *Jul 1966*
CIJE 8   RIE 16
SN   Description of the distribution of individuals or groups with reference to their social status
BT   Demography
RT   Incidence
     Social Class
     Social Mobility
     Social Status
     Social Stratification

Social Drinking
USE   DRINKING

●Concept represented by two or more USE terms in coordination

27   A page from the *ERIC Thesaurus*

information unit then these will be the only documentary sources that can be consulted for term generation. If it is an existing unit then these outside sources will be important to make sure that the thesaurus does not become so specialized that it ignores important general concepts.

It is important that individuals are involved in testing and generating terms for the thesaurus. This is particularly true in areas such as community information where the information content of the unit is often used to solve user problems that are in a totally different subject area. Term generation must therefore involve users and users' problems. A useful way of doing this is to use client enquiry sheets and generate terms from them in the same way as is done for the literature within the information unit. The terms generated from enquiry sheets can then be fed into the embryonic thesaurus.

The other group of individuals involved in the process are outside subject specialists who can be used to generate terms by getting from them lists of 'the 25 most important subject terms in your discipline at the moment'. This technique can be used with local professionals in areas such as law, accountancy, teaching or probation work.

This range of processes will generate a large number of terms over a period of several months, and will involve some complex and sometimes some philosophical discussions about the nature of the information unit, the type of clients that it will be serving and the level and the specificity of information that it contains.

As terms are generated and assembled, decisions will need to be made on relationships between terms. The basic broad terms of the subject field may have been identified early on, or they may have emerged as the thesaurus grew. By the end, however, an hierarchical map of the discipline should be apparent, consisting of broad groupings of processes, users, tactics and problems with links leading up and down and across within each of the broad groupings. It might be clear at this stage that there is a strong relationship between a thesaurus and a classification scheme which might result in a decision to go ahead and produce a linked thesaurus and classification scheme such as the proposed NACAB social welfare or the existing thesaurofacet from English Electric (see figures 32 and 33).

Whilst these links and relationships are being inserted into the thesaurus, decisions will need to be made on final house-styles of terms and an agreed format for the layout of the thesaurus. At this stage the British Standards Institution *Guidelines for the establish-*

Reproduced with the permission of Wetenschappelik en Technisch Documentatie en Informatik Centrum voor de Krigsmacht.

28 A page from the TDCK circular thesaurus system

ment and development of *multilingual thesauri* and the International Organisation for Standardisation *Documentation: Guidelines for the establishment and development of monolingual thesauri* will be extremely useful and will supplement the Aitchison and Gilchrist text.

A number of examples of different formats of thesauri is given (figures 26–29) and it can be seen that layout is very much a matter of personal preference. Simple typed sheets are quite acceptable, and the new word-processing packages on micros, such as WordWise and WordStar, allow quite sophisticated layouts with index terms in bold and the relationship structure in finer type. Manual production with typing always raises the problem of updating and insertion of new terms, which of course is easily overcome with the advent of word-processing packages with the complete thesaurus held on floppy disk. This allows regular modification to the vocabulary, with printouts taking place when the number of new terms suggests that another edition is required.

THE POST-COORDINATE APPROACH
Pre-coordinate indexes
The order of terms in the index string is a fundamental problem. The Western Australia system, alphabetical subject-headings lists and classification schemes all result in terms that have to be searched for in a particular order in the string. In the early enumerative classification schemes and alphabetical subject-headings lists this string was produced in a rather ad hoc fashion. However, in systems such as *Current Technology Index* and the Western Australia list the citation order is rigorous and it is possible for the searcher to work out the particular string required at the searching stage. However, in all of these systems it is the indexer who decides on the particular order of terms by applying some form of citation order. This approach is called a pre-coordinate one, in that an indexer is co-ordinating the order of terms in the index string at the input stage.

The problem which arises here is that many searchers will not match the particular citation order that the system has decreed. What happens if the citation order used by the indexing system does not match the multi-dimensional requirements of the searcher? Thus in the Western Australia thesaurus the concept **Research** was a common modifier added to any number of services or agents. Similarly, **Aborgines** are a client group normally synthesized to either

DIRR

IRRD-85

INFORMATION TECHNIQUES AND DOCUMENTATION

Automatic 9982

Traffic Control 0458

Operational Research 9055

Cybernetics

Program

Simulation

Analogue

Output Medium

Data Storage Medium

Terminology

Language

Computer

Data Bank

Data

Dictionary

Thesis

Data Processing

Classification

Steering 5185

State of the Art Report

Research Project

INFORMATION DOCUMENTATION

Conference

Text-Book

Activity Report

Report of Visit

Research Report

Patent

Translation

Lecture

Bibliography

Organisation (Association) 9057

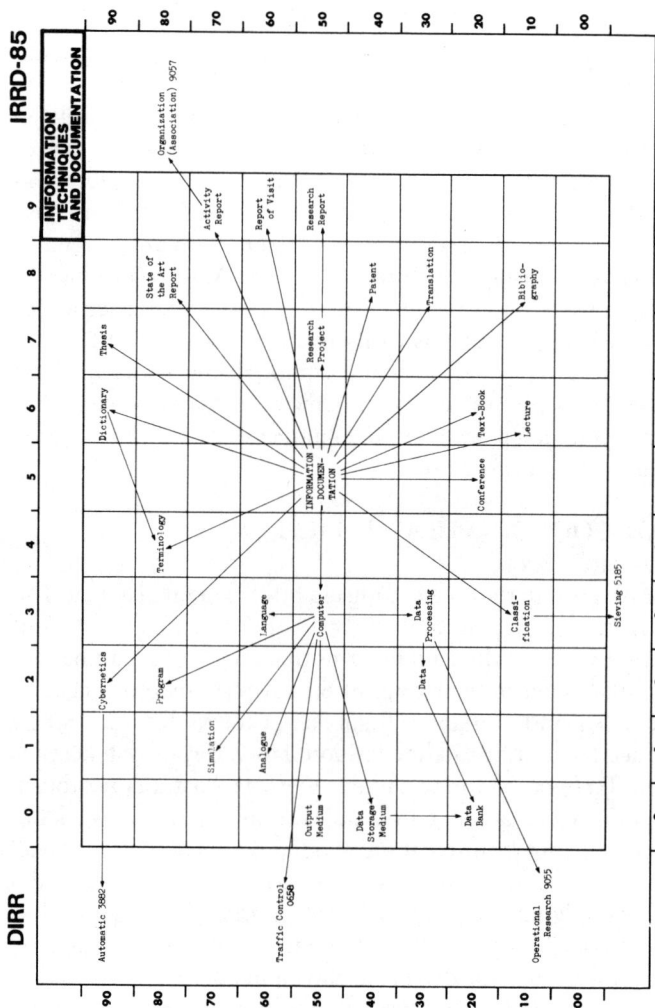

Reproduced with the permission of OECD.
29 A page from the *OECD International road research documentation thesaurus, 1972*

services or agents but occasionally standing on their own to represent general material. A searcher requiring all information on **Research relating to Aborigines** will need to spend a considerable amount of time working through all the service and agent terms that have had **Aborgines** synthesized to them followed by the concept **Research** in order to obtain high recall of relevant material. The entry **Aborigines/Research** will merely retrieve those aspects of research concerning Aborigines that do not relate to either services or agents. The problem is one of searching for concepts that the citation order may have either scattered or structured in such a way that it does not match the search requirements of the user.

Cycled and rotated indexes

Pre-coordinate systems are unable to cope with this particular problem. There are obviously ways of making large numbers of entries for each item, with each index term in the string being **cycled** round so that each term comes to the front, thus:

Unemployed/Research/Birmingham/Crisis counselling
Research/Birmingham/Crisis counselling/Unemployed
Birmingham/Crisis counselling/Unemployed/Research
Crisis counselling/Unemployed/Research/Birmingham

This system obviously ensures that each term in the string becomes an access point.

The disadvantage with cycled systems is that the original order of terms in the string is not retained, therefore the full sense of the string is sometimes lost. A **rotated** index retains the order of the index string but files each entry under a different word in the string.

Rotating can be done in two ways, firstly with the filing device being kept in the middle of the page so that the other terms can remain in their correct relative position. Thus if we indicate our four index terms using ABCD then the entries would have the following structure:

ABCD
ABCD
ABCD
ABCD

This process of identification and filing is best achieved using a computer (see figure 30), and there are microcomputer software pro-

```
DECENTRALIZED LIBRARY SYSTEMS
              LIBRARY TECHNICAL PROCESSES
              LIBRARY TECHNICIANS
        STATE LICENSING BOARDS
       FAMILY LIFE EDUCATION
         WORK LIFE EXPECTANCY
       FAMILY LIFE
       SOCIAL LIFE
              LIFTING
              LIGHT
              LIGHTED PLAYGROUNDS
              LIGHTING
     FLEXIBLE LIGHTING DESIGN
   TELEVISION LIGHTING
              LIGHTS
   TELEVISION LIGHTS
              LIMITED EXPERIENCE
       RAISED LINE DRAWINGS
              LINEAR PROGRAMING
              LINGALA
              LINGUISTIC COMPETENCE
              LINGUISTIC PATTERNS
              LINGUISTIC PERFORMANCE
              LINGUISTIC THEORY
              LINGUISTICS
      APPLIED LINGUISTICS
COMPUTATIONAL LINGUISTICS
  CONTRASTIVE LINGUISTICS
  DESCRIPTIVE LINGUISTICS
   DIACHRONIC LINGUISTICS
 MATHEMATICAL LINGUISTICS
   STRUCTURAL LINGUISTICS
    SYNCHRONIC LINGUISTICS
        CLEFT LIP
              LIPREADING
              LISTENING
              LISTENING COMPREHENSION
              LISTENING GROUPS
              LISTENING HABITS
              LISTENING SKILLS
```

30 Part of the rotated index from an in-house index produced at Birmingham Polytechnic

grams that will allow this to take place. Alternatively, a manual version of the same technique can be achieved by simply underlining the relevant part of the string with a red line and then instructing filers to file under that element. This technique is often used in the entering of synthesized Universal decimal classification classmarks into a classified catalogue thus:

A̲BCD

ABCD

AB̲CD

ABC̲D

Permutated indexes

Nonetheless the only way that it is possible to guarantee that every single term is linked together with every other possible term in the index string is to permutate fully the entire index string. True permutation means that there will be an entry into the system for every word combined with every single other word in the index. A fully permutated system such as this requires an enormous number of entry points, for there are technically 24 different combinations of four index terms, and there are 120 combinations of five different index terms. It is most unlikely that any user will require every single possible combination of index terms in order to guarantee that a particular search strategy is matched but even if we exclude a number of absurd combinations it will still require a very large number of access points in the system if every possible combination of relevant search strategies is to be matched.

It was this particular failure of pre-coordinate systems to match every possible combination of users' search strategies that led to the emergence of post-coordinate indexing systems.

Post-coordinate indexes

Post-coordinate indexing systems take a different approach to the problem of matching users' search strategies. The process of indexing is the same, and indeed a thesaurus or faceted classification scheme can be used. However, the indexer does not place the index terms into any particular citation order.

In order to produce an information-retrieval system that is searched in a post-coordinate fashion it is necessary to rethink the information-retrieval file. If we free ourselves from the concept of each *item* having an entry which carries a string of index terms and conceive instead of an entry for each *index term* which contains information about every item, then part of the problem is resolved.

The original manual post-coordinate systems designed in the 1960s were of this sort. Traditional 5 × 3 catalogue cards had headings taken from a thesaurus and on that card were written the accession numbers of all items which had been indexed using that term. Returning to that example from the Western Australian system there would have been a card with the heading **Aborigines**, a card with the heading **Research** and a card with the heading **Education**. Every time the concepts **Research, Aborigines** or **Education** were used as indexing terms the accession numbers of the docu-

ABORIGINES

0	1	2	3	4	5	6	7	8	9
20	11	22	13	14	25	36	7	18	29
60	31	62	63	74	85	66	57	48	59
80	81		83	104	125	116	97	88	99
	101		93		135	156	127		119
	131						147		
							167		

RESEARCH

0	1	2	3	4	5	6	7	8	9
10	31	2	43	24	15	16	37	18	39
40	71	52	73	54	65	26	87	98	89
110	81	72	123	84	105	66	137	118	159
	111	102		124		136	177	148	
		152		134					
				164					
				174					

31 Index cards from a manual post-coordinate index

ments were written on the relevant card. The resulting entries might have looked like figure 31:

It is now possible to search under **Research, Aborigines** or **Education** without any preconceived idea about a citation order or a structure of relationships. If the accession number of one particular document appears on all three of those index cards then the retrieval system is indicating a degree of relevance. It does not matter, though, whether **Aborigine** was taken out of the system first or last – all terms are deemed equally important.

Such a manual system obviously has some problems concerning the ease and speed of searching and it is clear at once that the system merely leads to an accession list which gives the full information about each document. However, it should be clear that the system is workable. It did not take long before the small 5 × 3 cards evolved into much larger optical coincidence cards, where, instead of writing the accession number of a document, a small hole is punched in the card on a large grid of accession numbers (see figure 32). This

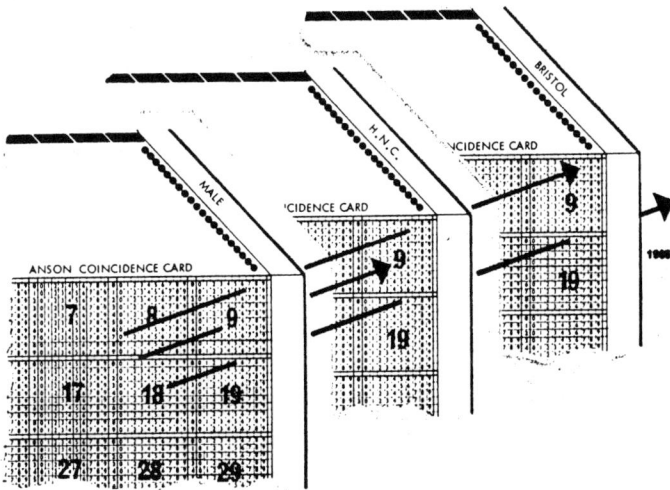

32 Optical coincidence cards

hole indicates that a document exists at that accession number which has been indexed using the term. If three or four cards are taken out of the filing cabinet and positioned on top of each other, light shining through a hole in all of the cards indicates that a document has been indexed using all those terms. It does not matter in which order the subject cards are placed on top of each other and therefore we are free of the need for citation orders. These optical coincidence cards were used extensively in specialized information units and a considerable number of school libraries and learning resource centres during the 1970s, allowing sophisticated search strategies to be used to retrieve information from highly specialized information stores.

The vocabularies used to produced post-coordinate indexes were normally thesauri of the type produced by the Library Board of Western Australia and they exist in a very wide range of different subject fields. Earlier sections in this chapter give some idea about the thesaurus in general and some indication of ways of producing such a tool.

Post-coordinate indexes of this manual type, whether optical coincidence or written accession number, are rather cumbersome to manage in that the punching process is time-consuming and the requirement for a separate accessions list is irritating for the user.

However, the advent of computer-based systems has transformed the whole approach to post-coordinate retrieval systems as it is relatively easy to set up the files required for post-coordinate searching. Chapter 6 on computers and information retrieval discusses the large bibliographic databases and smaller microcomputer systems all of which are primarily post-coordinate in their approach.

ALPHABETICAL APPROACHES
AND CLASSIFICATION SCHEMES

The alphabetical subject retrieval systems discussed so far range from the early alphabetical subject approaches using headings lists such as Sears, through the increased use of citation orders to arrange terms in strings, then to the use of a thesaurus to generate the original terms and from there to the use of post-coordinate matching processes which remove the need for the citation order.

We have been discussing the majority of information systems in terms of arranging items, or arranging catalogues or lists of those items. However, all these systems interrelate with each other in an important way. The role of citation orders in classification schemes, in alphabetical subject-headings lists and in pre-coordinate indexes based on thesauri means that the process of grouping into facets and the arrangement of concepts within facets and groups is of value in the design of classification schemes as well as thesauri.

Similarly, the alphabetical subject index to the classification scheme that translates a search strategy from the language of the problem into the artificial language of the classification scheme is a tool that can be produced using a number of different alphabetical subject-retrieval systems. Likewise, an index to a book given at the end of the text is produced using a specialist version of the alphabetical subject theories already identified. A number of book indexes have been produced using post-coordinate approaches, and the majority of such indexes use a simple natural-language catchword approach, with the resulting strings rotated around so that the important terms in the phrase become entry points in the index.

In a more specific way the printed schedules of classification schemes also need indexes to locate a particular concept in the schedules. We have already identified the thesaurus as a particularly useful way of showing in an alphabetical arrangement all the relationships between the concepts, and it ought to be possible to use a thesaurus as the index to the schedules of a classification scheme and

Teletypewriters

Telegraph receivers
Telegraph transmitters
BT(A) Automatic typewriters
Typewriters

Television   **NN**
RT   Television and radio manufacturing
     industries
     Television broadcasting
     Television films
     Television recording
     Television telephone calling
     apparatus
     Vehicular communications

Television Aerials   **NSN**
RT   Television masts
     Television receivers
     Television stations
     Television transmission systems
     Television transmitters
     Towers
BT(A) Television apparatus

**Television and Radio Manufacturing
Industries**   **ZKFW**
UF   Radio industry
RT   Radio
     Television

Television Apparatus   **NJ**
RT   Television switching
NT(A) Colour television apparatus
     Fluorescent screens
     Radiofrequency transformers
     Telecine equipment
     Television aerials
     Television receivers
     Television recording cameras
     Television telephone calling
     apparatus
     Television transmitters
     Vision mixers

Equalising pulses
Horizontal deflection oscillators
Limiters
Phase detectors
Scanning circuits
Synchronising pulse generators
Synchronising separators
Television time bases
Vertical deflection oscillators
Videofrequency amplifiers
Vision mixers

Television Colour Camera Tubes   MCI
UF   Colour camera tubes (television)
     Colour cell
     Pick up tubes (colour television)
     Plumbicons
RT   Colour television cameras
BT(A) Colour television apparatus

Television Colour Picture Tubes   MCO
UF   Apple tubes
     Banana tubes
     Colour picture tubes (television)
     Chromatrons
     Display tubes (television colour)
     Flat picture tubes
     Gabor tubes
     Kaiser Aiten thin tubes
     Kinescope (colour)
     Reflected beam kinescope
     Shadowmask tubes
     Television display tubes (colour)
RT   Colour television receivers

Television Communication Systems *use*
Television Transmission Systems

Television Display Tubes (colour) *use*
Television Colour Picture Tubes

Television Distribution Systems *use*
Television Transmission Systems

Reproduced with the permission of J Aitchison and English Electric.
33 An extract from the thesaurus portion of the *Thesaurofacet*

at the same time allow the classification schedules to give a structured, relational approach to the same concepts that appear alphabetically in the thesaurus. Such a tool has been in existence for several years, called a 'thesaurofacet' and published by the English Electric Company (see figures 33 and 34). It is interesting that the new social welfare classification scheme being produced by the National Association of Citizens' Advice Bureaux is being perceived as a linked thesaurus and faceted classification scheme. An example of both parts from the English Electric thesaurofacet is given in figures 33 and 34 and it can be seen that the two parts of the retrieval

126 *Organizing information: principles and practice*

vocabulary have a creative relationship with each other with movement between the thesaurus and the classification scheme being effected through the notation.

Electron tubes   MA   96

MBE	**Electron wave tubes**		· Electron tube oscillators LL MA	
MBF	Travelling wave tubes		· Electron tube rectifiers JPL	
MBH	Backward wave tubes			
MBJ	Carcinotrons		**By components:**	
MBM	Magnetrons			
MBP	Velocity modulated tubes	MF	Electron tube components	
MBQ	Klystrons		· Electrodes KP	
MBT	**Electron beam deflection tubes**		· Electron guns EHT	
MBV	Indicator tubes (tuning)		· Electron lenses EHL	
MBW	Trochotrons		· Fluorescent screens DWQ	
MC	Cathode ray tubes	MF3	Grids (tube components)	
MC2	Image converter tubes	MF5	Filaments (tube components)	
MC4	Image intensifiers	MF6	Heaters (tube components)	
MC6	Storage tubes			
MCE	Television camera tubes		**By techniques:**	
MCI	Television colour camera tubes			
MCL	Television picture tubes	MFM	Electron tube production techniques	
MCO	Television colour picture tubes		*Combine with appropriate notation from Production engineering and other schedules*	
MCQ	**X ray tubes**		· Brazing TQ	
MCS	**Phototubes**		· Glass metal seals QNS	
MCT	Photomultipliers		· Soldering TQO	
MCW	**Electron multipliers**		· Vacuum engineering PV	
	· Photomultipliers MCT		· Welding TN	
	By number of electrodes:			
MD	Diodes (tubes)	MG	*Semiconductors*	
	· Plasma diodes (tubes) MAR		· Crystals FB	
MD3	Triodes (tubes)		· Semiconductor physics EKH	
	· Thyratrons MAI			
MD5	Multielectrode tubes	MG2	**SEMICONDUCTOR MATERIALS**	
	· Trochotrons MBW	MGB	Binary semiconductor materials	
MD6	Phasitrons	MGC	Ternary semiconductor materials	
MD7	Reactance tubes	MGF	Intrinsic semiconductor materials	
MDA	Tetrodes	MGG	Extrinsic semiconductor materials	
MDB	Dynatrons	MGJ	Impurity elements	
MDC	Resnatrons	MGK	Acceptors	
MDG	Pentodes	MGL	Donors	
MDH	Pentagrid converters	MGN	N type semiconductor materials	
MDL	Multiple unit tubes	MGP	P type semiconductor materials	
		MGR	Bulk semiconductor materials	
	By application:	MGS	Multivalley semiconductor materials	
		MGV	Mixed valence semiconductor materials	
	· Storage tubes MC6			
	· Television camera tubes MCE	MGW	Semiinsulators	
	· Television picture tubes MCL		*For individual semiconductor materials combine with the notation from the materials schedules.*	
MER	Counting tubes		*for example:—*	
	· Indicator tubes (numerical) MB7	MG2/GLR	Silicon semiconductor materials	
	· Trochotrons MBW	MG2/GLS	Germanium semiconductor materials	
MET	Dekatrons	MG2/HFG/HLP	Gallium arsenide semiconductor materials	
	For other applications combine notation for Electron tube with application For manual systems the preferred order is application followed by tube, but permuted entries may be made, for example —	MH	**SEMICONDUCTOR DEVICES**	
	· Electron tube amplifiers LE/MA		· Semiconductor amplifiers LE/MH	
	· Electron tube demodulators LW/MA		· Semiconductor demodulators LW/MH	
	· Electron tube mixers LX/MA		· Semiconductor lasers MOF	
	· Electron tube modulators LV/MA		· Semiconductor masers MNL	
			· Semiconductor modulators LV/MH	

Reproduced with the permission of J Aitchison and English Electric.
34 A page from faceted classification portion of the *Thesaurofacet*

Chain Indexing

Two other particular indexing systems have been employed to link classification schemes to the real language in which users formulate their search strategies. Chain indexing and PRECIS indexing are techniques that are used primarily to produce the subject indexes to classified arrangements. They are in fact systems that have efficient and useful citation orders so that index strings can be manipulated with the minimum of cost and maximum user gain. They are therefore systems which are also used in producing the headings and reference structures in other pre-coordinate alphabetical retrieval systems.

Chain indexing was developed by Ranganathan, the classification theorist who did most of the early work on analytico-synthetic approaches to classification. Chain indexing is an extremely cost-effective way of producing a very limited number of entries to translate a search strategy into the notation of the classification scheme.

A chain index assumes that the classification scheme groups related concepts into classes and these classes are subdivided from general to specific. Thus if a user enters a classified arrangement at a broad subject such as **literature,** the classified arrangement itself will lead the searcher from the general concept of **literature** down to a required concept such as **romantic English poetry**. The chain index, therefore, does not duplicate that process. An item on **sixteenth-century romantic English poetry** is assigned the classmark in the Dewey decimal classification of **821.3**. This index string will be entered in the chain index in the following way:

Romantic: 16th century: Poetry: English: Literature 821.3

The other index entries will then be structured in the following way:

16th century: Poetry: English: Literature 821.3
Poetry: English: Literature 821
English Literature 820
Literature 800

The interesting thing here is that each term in the original string has become an access point in the subject index, but as the terms get broader and broader they lead to the broad classmarks. Thus a searcher accessing under **Literature** for a required search concept **Romantic English poetry** will merely pick up the notation **800** and will need to go to the classified file to search from **800** down through the classified sequence to the specific concept **Romantic English poetry**. This means that as soon as the first book on **English literature** comes into the system the index entry **Literature 800** is made, and need never be made again. **Literature** will not be in the subject index sub-divided by any specific term, and therefore however many books come into the system concerned with specific aspects of English literature this one subject access point **Literature 800** will stand for every item in the system within that main class. Thus the entry points **English, Poetry** and **Literature** made for this specific item will stand for a wide range of other items in the system that may be classified at more specific classmarks. The system is thus extremely economical, resulting in very few new index entries having to be made apart from the highly specialized terms. The system works on the assumption that the user knows how to browse down through the classified arrangement.

Thus we have an indexing system that gets its citation order from the classification scheme itself and is from specific to general. Instead of rotating all of these terms around, as we saw in a rotated or cycled index, the system merely drops off each specific term in turn so that each term becomes an entry point but the string itself becomes shorter and shorter. Each string leads to a broader and broader classmark ending finally with the main class number itself. The system is designed to work with faceted classification schemes with rigorous citation orders, but it can be made to work reasonably effectively in enumerative classification schemes with some minor modifications.

Although chain indexes are extremely efficient in terms of the number of entries made, they fail if the searcher does not grasp the key point about having to search down through the hierarchy of the classified arrangement to find the specific item. Thus someone wanting **Romantic English poetry** and looking under the general concept of **Literature** will see no other index entries under **Literature** except that general one. It is possible that the searcher may think that the information unit has only got general information on **Literature**, whereas it is intended that the searcher recognizes the need to go into the classified file at 800 and browse down through the hierarchical arrangement.

This system of subject indexing was used by the *British National Bibliography* for many years, and is still the major method of producing such indexes to the classified catalogues of public and academic libraries. It was the worry that the system may not be working to the satisfaction of the user that resulted in the PRECIS indexing system being introduced by *BNB*.

PRECIS indexing
(preserved context indexing system)

The PRECIS indexing system was adopted by the *British National Bibliography* after it became clear that the chain-indexing system used to generate the subject index was no longer satisfactory. It was recognized that the system to replace chain indexing had to be capable of producing co-extensive strings of index terms that covered the full subject content of each item, and that each co-extensive string had to be accessible by the user at each access point in the subject index. It was also felt that each index string had to be meaningful to the user and at the same time the process had to be as mechanized as possible.

PRECIS is therefore a sophisticated alphabetical system which involves the use of shunting in order to show the relationships between the various terms in the index string. This shunting process is based on different relationships that exist between the terms in the string rather than on some purely clerical process of rotating terms round that we saw in the rotated or cycled indexes.

The index uses a two-line structure, with the first line containing the lead term, which is the access point the user goes into the system at, followed on the same line by a qualifier term. On the line below are the other terms in the string which are called display terms. This two-line approach allows the lead term to be linked to two possible other terms in the string, the qualifier and the display, rather than having to be linked solely to the one term that follows it in the string. In order to ensure that each lead term or access point is linked to the qualifier and display terms in a meaningful way the order of the shunting around of the terms is modified depending on the type of term that exists in the string. The type of term is decided at the indexing stage, when each one is assigned a particular operator which the computer program recognizes and this produces shunted indexing strings which retain their meaning through this use of differing orders of terms. Thus:

States
Size. Effects on Democracy

Size. States
Effects on Democracy

Democracy
Effects of Size of State

We can see here that the two-line approach allows the access point **size** to be linked to both **states** and **effects on democracy**, and at the same time the entry under **democracy** modifies the order of the string considerably to ensure that meaning is retained. Similarly:

Society. Great Britain
Role of military forces

British military forces
Role in society

Here again we can see that the access point or lead term **society** is linked to both **Great Britain** and the **Role of military forces**, and that the entry under **British military forces** restructures the indexing string to retain the full meaning.

PRECIS is a very powerful indexing system, and the extract from *BNB* (figure 35) shows how the two-line shunting approach with the modification in the order of terms allows a far more creative searching tool than the chain index discussed earlier or the cycled or rotated indexes that might have been available as an alternative. However, the rather complex use of operators and the necessity in a large subject index to have access to computer software which is not readily available means that PRECIS indexing on this large scale is difficult. However, a number of libraries have produced very reasonable PRECIS index approaches using terms taken from their own thesaurus and manually modifying the shunting order to retain meaning. The idea of a two-line index layout to retain links between effectively three terms at the same time is an important factor in the user satisfaction.

CATCHWORD INDEXING

The process of indexing or assigning subject strings to describe documents can be an entirely creative ad hoc process. Many information units use retrieval systems that involve alphabetical subject headings generated by individuals expressed in terms that they think their users might find valuable. Alternatively, a classification

Social economics	330.15'5
Social education	370.11'5
Social education. Adolescents. England	
— *Reports, surveys*	370.11'5
Social education. Secondary schools. England	
Projects: Schools Council Social Education Project —	
Reports, surveys	370.11'5
Social environment	
See also	
Home environment	
Social environment. Adolescents. Great Britain	
Effects on attitudes to politics in Great Britain	
301.15'43'320942085	
Social environment. Children, 7-9 years. Great Britain	
Effects on development of writing skills — *Reports,*	
surveys	372.6'23
Social ethics	
— *Readings*	170
— *Readings — Secondary school texts*	170
Social ethics. Great Britain	
1700-1900	170
Social ethics. Special themes. Tragedies. Shakespeare,	
William. Drama in English	822.3'3
Social factors	
See also	
Bisocial factors	
Ethnic factors	
Psychosocial factors	
Socioeconomic factors	
Sociological factors	
Social factors. Academic achievement. Students. Secondary	
schools. Manchester. Lancashire	
— *Reports, surveys*	373.1'2'64
Social factors. Coronary diseases. Heart. Man	616.1'23'071
Social factors. Development. Children. United States	
— *Reviews of research*	155.4'0973
Social factors. Elections. Members. Great Britain.	
Parliament. House of Commons	
1832-1872	329'.023'42081
Social factors. Genetics. Man	
— *Conference proceedings*	573.2'1
Social factors. Health. Man	613
Social factors. Juvenile delinquency. Urban regions.	
England	
— *Study examples: Boys, 8-18 years — Study regions:*	
London	364.2'5
Social factors. Primary education. England	
— *Study regions: England. Midlands — Reports, surveys*	
372.9'424	

Reproduced with the permission of the British Library.

35 An extract from the subject index from the *British National Bibliography*

scheme might be used and the alphabetical subject index to that classification scheme is produced using a similar ad hoc process. Such a system lacks many rules or a consistency of approach either in choice of words used or in the order into which words are combined together. Much book indexing falls into this category, which is often called catchword indexing.

The alphabetical subject index to the Citizens' Advice Bureaux (old) information system is an excellent example of such an approach. Entries include:

Supplementary benefit 9.2.14
Supplementary benefit: what it is and who can claim 9.2.14.3
Couples, which partner should claim 9.2.14.3
Housing costs which are paid by supplementary benefit 9.2.14.5

Some of these entries might also be re-structured and entered under different access points in the subject index, but on the whole the process is seen as a creative way of communicating with the searcher (see also figure 36).

It is often suggested that this sort of uncontrolled device means that neither the indexer nor the searcher are able to identify and agree the words that will be access points to the system. Natural-language indexing allows a retrieval system to exist without a controlled vocabulary, but systematic natural-language indexing will use all or most of the words that appear in a title and an abstract as legitimate access points and will normally involve the use of computerized databases for searching. Thus as soon as a system moves away from using every word in the title and abstract the user needs to be able to work out which words have and which words have not been used as access points to a particular document. In order to agree on this a vocabulary will generally be needed.

Ad hoc catchword systems also lack a structure to the order of terms in an index string. This is the problem of combination order or citation order. Simple rules of thumb such as 'prefer the order used by searchers', 'do not invert or change the order of everyday usage' may sound reasonable when applied to multi-term concepts such as **Housing benefit** or **Housing for the elderly**. However, if these terms were inverted **Benefit, housing** it would ensure that the items were entered in the system very close to **Benefit, supplementary** and **Benefit, unemployment**. Similarly, inverting **Housing for the elderly** to produce **Elderly, housing** allows the information retrieval system to bring together material about the elderly. Thus the decision to invert the string is essentially a citation order decision, and once made should be consistently applied.

Ad hoc catchword indexing, however creative, will tend to fail on the two counts of vocabulary control and citation order once the index becomes large. At some stage there will need to be produced a

SUPPLEMENTARY BENEFIT   CARD II

How to claim supplementary benefit   9.2.14.10

Fares to the DHSS   office   9.2.14.10.

Backdated claims for supplementary benefit   9.2.14.10.

How and when supplementary benefit is paid   9.2.14.10.

Form B1: for unemployed people claiming
                       supplementary benefit   9.2.14.12.

Form A14N: statement of supplementary benefit
                                 entitlement   9.2.14.13.

Form A124: checking assessment of supplementary
                                       benefit   9.2.14.14.

Cohabitation rule   CPAG handbook

Availability for work   CPAG Handbook

Students and supplementary benefit   9.2.14.35.

SUPPLEMENTARY BENEFIT

Reproduced with the permission of NACAB.

36 An example of the subject index cards of the (old) NACAB information system

list of terms used and a set of principles about combining terms into a particular order. Small indexes can survive following ad hoc catch-word principles, and many book indexes are extraordinarily successful when produced in this fashion. Many book indexers feel that the process is an art rather than a technique, but it is the small size and the ease of scanning a printed book index which allows catch-word indexing to flourish.

6   Computerized retrieval systems

NATURAL-LANGUAGE INDEXING

The advent of computers in the information-retrieval process meant that the post-coordinate approach became easier and the growth in on-line bibliographic databases searched through terminals in a post-coordinate fashion is witness to the success of that process. However, computers also brought about another change in the indexing system.

All the information-retrieval processes that we have discussed so far have assumed that an indexer is intellectually involved in the process of identifying what a particular item is actually about and then, having decided what it is about, trying to describe it using terms taken from a controlled vocabulary – be it classification scheme, thesaurus or alphabetical subject-headings list. We have shown that by so doing the searcher is helped in terms of synonym control, homonym control and an indication of the relationships that exist between concepts. We have indicated that this indexing process of using terms from a controlled vocabulary to describe the subject content of an item is advantageous to the user in that it ensures consistency and brings together related items for the searcher irrespective of the words and phrases that an author might use in the text. These systems are called assigned-term systems, because an indexer actually assigns terms to describe each item.

There is an alternative methodology which removes the indexer from this process. If the information that we have for each item in the system includes a title and an abstract then it is possible to assume that all the important words in the title and the abstract between them give an indication of the subject content of the item. If these terms are lifted out from the title and the abstract and are used as indexing terms then we have produced a derived-term indexing system. This uses a natural language or uncontrolled vocabulary based entirely on the words that the author used in the title and the abstract. The result is that each item has an indexing string which consists of far more terms than might have been used by an indexer and in the large bibliographic databases these are searched in a post-coordinate fashion.

In the majority of databases that are available for on-line searching, such as that provided by the Lockheed Dialog host service, or the growing number of UK services such as POLIS, the House of Commons Library's database, and ACCOMPLINE the ex-GLC planning database, the indexing is of this derived-term natural-language type. It is post-coordinate, so that if a word is typed in at the terminal by a searcher the system responds by identifying the total number of items that exist that have used that particular term in either the title or the abstract. If a second term is then typed in the system can indicate the number of documents which have had both those indexing terms used in their titles or abstracts. The system is post-coordinate because it does not matter in which order the terms are entered into the system.

We can build up sophisticated search strategies using a technique called 'Boolean search logic' which allows us to indicate the relationship between terms in the search strategy. Thus if we enter terms using the link **AND** then we are searching for items in which both the terms have been used in the title or the abstract. If we then enter a third term linking it with an **AND** then we retrieve documents in which all three terms have been used in the title or the abstract. This is obviously a searching device which increases the specificity of the search and will therefore reduce the number of items that are relevant to ensure the greatest precision for the user. Many systems allow us to specify how far apart these three words must appear in the actual text of the abstract. Thus if we want the three search terms to be two or three words apart in the abstract we can so specify. An alternative logical relationship in the search strategy is to search for term A **OR** term B **OR** Term C. This will retrieve items which have any of the three search terms in that title or abstract. The total number of such items will be considerably more than in the previous search strategy where all three terms had to appear together in the text. This search strategy will obviously retrieve more items than the previous one and, because the search strategy is less specific, there will be a greater number of less relevant items. This search strategy is obviously increasing the recall for the searcher, and the resulting precision will be appreciably less. A final search strategy involves the use of the **NOT** logical relationship which allows us to exclude particular terms. This means that we will not retrieve any items that include that particular term in the title or the abstract. The three operators **AND, OR, NOT** allow us to construct fairly sophisticated search strategies linking long series of terms together using any of the three operators. By so doing users are controlling the particular recall and precision that the retrieval system is giving.

This Boolean searching approach is in no way confined to computer-based derived-term natural-language systems, as it is effectively how all searching on retrieval systems takes place. Early manual post-coordinate indexes gave impetus to the presentation of search strategies in this format and this was then developed further by the computer-based systems. The concepts of inclusion and exclusion are integral to the whole idea of classification schemes and other retrieval systems but it is obviously easier to perceive the process working when we are searching on-line databases.

Derived term index (KWIC and KWOC)
The idea of derived-term natural-language retrieval systems is seen in its full flowering when titles and abstracts are used together in the large bibliographic on-line systems. However, computers have been used to produce simple derived-term indexes based on titles alone. These indexes can lead to either classmarks or accession numbers. The computer merely rotates the title around so that every keyword in the title string becomes an entry point into the index. There are numerous minor modifications to the rotational principle, but the majority are either 'keyword-in-context' (KWIC) or 'keyword-out-of-context' (KWOC).

In the former case the significant entry point is kept in the middle of the page, so that the other words in the title are on both the left and the right of each particular keyword. This means that the searcher can look down the middle of the page and see an alphabetical listing of each keyword in the title surrounded by all the other words in the title (see figure 37). If there are six relevant words in the title, there will be six entries in the index, each one of them at a different alphabetical place in the sequence. Keyword-out-of-context indexes are a similar approach but in a rather traditional format, with each keyword taken out of the title and filed on the left-hand side in the

```
# STRESS DETERMINATION IN UNDERGROUND      EXCAVATIONS.  CONGRESS, DISCUSSION. 1F. =                               10873
# STABILITY OF ROCK SLOPES AND UNDERGROUND EXCAVATIONS.  CONTRIBUTIONS TO THE JOSEF STINI COLLOQUIUM,115F. =      03324
# THE DESIGN OF UNDERGROUND                EXCAVATIONS.  IN FAILURF AND BREAKAGE OF ROCK. ED. BY C.FAIRHURS        00113
HE MEASUREMENT OF GROUND DISPLACEMENT AROUND DEEP EXCAVATIONS. IN FIELD INSTRUMENTATION IN GEOTECH.=?             10182
ECMANICS STABILITY OF ROCK SLOPES AND UNDERGROUND EXCAVATIONS. IN GERMAN. 21ST=?                                 11971
PREVENTION OF SUDDEN INRUSH OF WATER INTO MINING EXCAVATIONS. IN RUSSIAN WITH ABRIDGED ENGLISH TABLE OF=?        12483
ON THE STRENGTH OF ROCKS SURROUNDING UNDERGROUND EXCAVATIONS. IN RUSSIAN. 13R. # EFFECT OF MOISTURE AND FREEZING 11250
ROCKS FORMING THE CEILINGS OF COOLED UNDERGROUND EXCAVATIONS. IN RUSSIAN. 5R. = ???????? THERMAL FRACTURING OF   11226
# LATERAL SUPPORT OF DEEP                  EXCAVATIONS.  IN SYMPOSIUM ON GROUND ENGINEERING, LONDON, JUNE 1       03383
970.13F,21R. = # THERMAL                   EXCAVATIONS.  IN SYMPOSIUM ON=? SEMISTIFF SHELL AS MEANS FOR THE       03330
EMPIRICAL SCIENTIFIC DIMENSIONING OF UNDERGROUND EXCAVATIONS. JET CUTTING=?  # SOME EXPERIMENTS ON THE AP         00078
PLICATION OF HIGH PRESSURE WATER JETS FOR MINERAL EXCAVATIONS. PART 2.                                           08019
# STRESS DETERMINATION AROUND MINING       EXCAVATIONS.  PROC. SYMPOSIUM ON ROCK MECH. DHANBAD, INDIA, JULY       10545
1972. 4F,3R. = # STABILITY OF ROCK SLOPES AND EXCAVATIONS.  PROGRESS REPORT. 13F,20R. =                          11447
# LARGE UNDERGROUND                        EXCAVATIONS.  REPORT. =                                                 02891
# THE FRACTURE OF BRITTLE ROCKS AROUND MINE EXCAVATIONS. REPORT. IN ADVANCES IN ROCK MECHANICS V1 PART B,.1       12630
N=? # ROCK MECHANICS PROBLEMS OF UNDERGROUND EXCAVATIONS. SALZBURG,1968.=?????? ON SHEARING JOINTS. IN SYMP       03325
OSIUM ON STABILITY OF ROCK SLOPES AND UNDERGROUND EXCAVATIONS. SEISMIC EVENTS.6F,27R. =                          07961
LENT DEFORMATION OF ROCK NEAR DEEP LEVEL. TABULAR EXCAVATIONS. SYMPOSIUM.7F,5R. =# ISOTROPIC AND ANISOTROPIC PLAS 01948
TIC YIELD ASSOCIATED WITH CYLINDRICAL UNDERGROUND EXCAVATIONS. SYMPOSIUM. =                                      02980
# LATERAL SUPPORT OF DEEP                  EXCAVATIONS.  SYMPOSIUM. IN STABILITY OF ROCK SLOPES. 8F,25R. =         10078
REMENT OF STRESS IN THE GROUND SURROUNDING MINING EXCAVATIONS.FACTORS GOVERNING THE DESIGN OF STRAIN CELL=# MEASU 00336
                                                                                             # THREE-            13798
# SLOPE ANALYSIS FOR EXPLOSIVE             EXCAVATIONS.MEASUR.AT COAL PILLARS.9F,5R. =     # MEASU                10444
DIMENSIONAL DEFORMATION DURING SUPERFICIAL TUNNEL EXCAVATIONS. REPORT.47F. =                                     06411
REMENT OF STRESS IN THE GROUND SURROUNDING MINING EXCAVATIONS.REPORT.IN FRENCH.4F.=? RECOMMENDATIONS ON WORK DONE 12125
OF IMPENDING ROCK FAILURE FOR SAFTY IN MINES AND EXCAVATIONS. # EARLY WARNING SYSTEM                             12170
USING INJECTED CONCRETE-SHOTCRETE IN UNDERGROUND EXCAVATIONS.TRANSL OF SHACHTNOE=?? IN THE INVESTIGATION OF THE   08727
STRESS-STRAIN STATE AROUND HORIZONTAL UNDERGROUND EXCAVATORS.IN RUSSIAN. =                                       08282
# CUTTING HARD ROCK WITH BUCKET            EXCAVATORS.  IN SERBO-CROAT. 3 YUGOSLAV.=# LABORATORY AND IN-SITU       03101
DETERMINATION OF CUTTING RESISTANCE USING ROTARY EXCAVATORS.                                                     07182
# FINITE ELEMENT MODEL IS                  EXCELLENT   PIT DESIGN TOOL. =                                         00478
# EXPERIMENTAL INVESTIGATIONS OF HEAT      EXCHANGES   IN FROZEN ROCKS. TEXTBOOK, IN RUSSIAN.                     13795
# THE                                      EXCITATION  FUNCTION OF A SPHERICAL DETONATION EMITTER. =              05398
# ROCK MECHANICS. THE AMERICAL NORTHWEST. AN EXECUTION GUIDE PREPARED FOR THE 3RD INT.CONGR.ISRM.=                02754
OR THE DAMS OF THE DRAU POWER STATIONS EDLING=? EXECUTION AND EFFECTIVENESS OF THE WATERTIGHT SUBSOIL SEALING F   12126
US OBTAINED IN ROCK MASSES=? # THE INFLUENCE OF EXECUTION AND THE MEASUREMENT METHOD ON THE DEFORMABILITY MODUL
THODS. REPORT. IN=? # PROCEDURES OF TUNNELLING EXECUTION USING THE NEW AUSTRIAN METHOD OR ANY OTHER SIMILAR ME
```

Reprinted with the permission of Pergamon Press.
37 An example from the *KWIC Index of rock-mechanics literature* by J P Jenkins and E T Brown

normal position followed by the rest of the title in its normal order. KWIC and KWOC indexes are very cheap methods of producing speedy indexes to collections as long as one has access to a reasonably sized computer and the relevant software. Several agencies are able to do this, and the Association for Information Management (ASLIB) would be able to give advice on particular agencies.

These sorts of 'cheap and dirty' indexing systems have never been regarded very highly by the traditional library profession but research at Bath University has suggested that they can be extremely useful for particular sorts of users who require reasonably high precision in indexes that need to be produced very quickly.

Citation indexes

An interesting variation on derived-term indexes has been the emergence of citation indexes. Although totally beyond the scope of a small information unit to produce, their availability through on-line database hosts such as Lockheed Dialog means that searchers need to be aware of their capabilities. At the end of most articles and research reports authors will give a list of references to other items that have been relevant in writing the article. If a number of different articles are cited in one particular item there is a reasonable possibility that the articles are in some way linked. Citation indexes, therefore, allow a user to identify all those articles which have cited a particular single article during the course of the year. If the searcher can increase the specificity of a search by identifying those articles which have cited two or even three key items during the year then the chances are that the precision of the search and the resulting relevance of the output are both increasing.

The interesting thing about citation indexes is that they remove any reliance on language and the meanings of words. They are based entirely on the assumption that if authors cite other authors then there is a relationship, however tenuous, between them. Databases such as the *Social Science Citations Index* (see figure 38) can be searched on-line through the Lockheed Dialog host system and can allow powerful searching strategies to be formulated in areas where high recall and poor terminology occur together.

Problems associated with natural language systems

Derived-term indexing systems can be extremely satisfactory, particularly where full abstracts are used to produce the natural

HOCHREICH D — VOL PG YR

```
75 J PERS SOC PSYCHOL  32 540
   HOCHREIC.DJ   J CONS CLIN    N   46  177 78
75 J CONSULT CLIN PSYCH  43 273
   DEVINE RC    J PSYCHOL           98   75 78
HOCHSCHILD AR
73 AM J SOCIOL  78 1011
   BALLOU PK    SIGNS          R   3  436 77
HOCHSCHILD A
73 ANNALS NY ACAD SCI 208 179
   WHITFIEL.MD  CAN PSYCHI        23    9 78
75 AM SOCIOL REV  40 553
   MINDEL CH    J GERONTOL        33  103 78
76 CRISIS AM I  251
   GADLIN H    J SOC HIST         11  305 78
HOCHSCHILD AR
73 CHANGING WOMEN CHANG  258
   GREENBLA.CS  SIGNS         R   3  622 78
75 ANOTHER VOICE  280
   GOULD M    AM SOCIOL          12  182 77
HOCHSCHILD G
65 STRUCTURE LIE GROUPS
   DJOKOVIC DZ  MATH Z           158   99 78
HOCHSCHILD R
71 EXP GERONTOL  6 113
   NANDY K    J AM GER SO        26   74 78
73 EXP GERONT  8 177
   SAMORAJS.T   PHARMACOL         16   36 78
73 EXP GERONTOL  8 185
   SAMORAJS.T   GERONTOLOGY       24   43 78
            PHARMACOL             16   36 78
73 J EXP GERONTOL  8 177
   NANDY K    J AM GER SO        26   74 78
HOCHSTEIN FA
57 J AM CHEMICAL SOC  79 5735
   SALUNKHE DK  CRC C R F S  R    9  265 77
HOCHSTEIN HD
73 B PARENTERAL DRUG AS  27 139
   BARRY DW   J INFEC DIS        136 5407 77
HOCHSTEIN S
76 J PHYSIOLOGY  262 237
   GAFNI H    BIOL CYBERN        28   73 77
   LEGGE GE    VISION RES        18   69 78
   MACLEOD DIA  ANN R PSYCH  R   29  613 78
76 J PHYSIOLOGY  262 265
   LEGGE GE    VISION RES        18   69 78
   MACLEOD DIA  ANN R PSYCH  R   29  613 78
HOCHSTEINMINTZE.V
72 ZBL BAKT I  156   1
72 ZBL BAKT I  156  15
72 ZBL BAKT HYG I ORI B  156  30
   VOROBIEV AA  ZH MIKROB I      1978   12 78
HOCHSTETTER N
59 P R VIRCHOW MED SOC  18 116
   HAGNELL O    NEUROPSYCHB        4  180 78
HOCHSTIM JR
67 J AM STAT ASSOC  62 976
   BOICE JD   AM J EPIDEM       107  127 78
70 PUBLIC OPIN QUART  34  69
   BOICE JD   AM J EPIDEM       107  127 78
   KOENIG DJ  CAN R SOC A   N   14  432 77
HOCHULI E
59 SCHWEIZ MED WSCHR  89 934
   NEME B    ACT OBST SC        57   19 78
HOCHWALD W
73 J ECONOMIC ISSUE MAR   57
   SAMUELS WJ  J ECON ISS        12   23 78
HOCK H
73 PERCEPT PSYCHOPHYS  13 116
   SCHULZ T    PSYCHOL BE        20   72 78
HOCK HS
70 J EXP PSYCHOLOGY  83 299
   SCHULZ T    PSYCHOL BE        20   72 78
HOCK K
76 GRUPPENPSYCHOTHERAPI
   LINK M    DYNAM PSYCH   B    11   79 78
76 NEUROSENLEHRE PSYCHO
   DETTMERI.   PRAX PSYCH    B    22  280 77
HOCK R
75 COLLEGE RESEARCH LIB  36 208
   HITCHING.KE  DREXEL LIBR       13   52 77
HOCK RA
77 BIOLOGICAL PSYCHOLOG  12 593
   HOCK RA    GROUP PSY P        30  108 77
HOCKADAY JM
65 ELECTROEN CLIN NEURO  18 575
   ANDRIOLA MR  GERIATRICS        33   59 78
HOCKE GR
57 WELT LABYRINTH
   ARNHEIM R    ART PSYCHOT        4  113 77
```

HOCKING WE — VOL PG YR

```
54 EXPT EDUCATION WHAT  242
54 PHILOSOPHY PHENOMENO  15 429
54 PHILOSOPHY PHENOMENO  15 446
   STURM D    J RELIG            58   13 78
HOCKMAN CH
60 AM HEART J  71 695
   DESILVA RA  AM HEART J        95  197 78
64 ELECTROEN CLIN NEURO  17 420
   FRENK H    BRAIN RES B         3    1 78
HOCKSTRA DJ
73 156 STANF U DEP OP R
76 COMPUT BIOMED RES   9 205
   TAUTU P    METH INF M        17    1 78
HODAPP R
77 COMMUNICATION
   MCCONNAU.PJ  UNIV IL LAW      1977 1113 77
HODAPP WJ
76 SOCIAL PRESCRIPTION
   MOORE SR    J DRUG EDUC        7  337 78
HODAS D
76 BUSINESS CAREER M TA
   SALSBURY S   J AM HIST    B   64  789 77
HODAS DP
76 BUSINESS CAREER M TA
   MAYO EL    TECHNOL CUL   B    19  123 78
HODDER BW
65 SCOTTISH GEOGRAPHICA  81  51
   OBUDHO RA  CAH ETUD AF       16  553 76
65 T I BRIT GEOGRAPHERS  36  97
   KEIL DE    J ANTHR RES       33  258 77
65 T PAPERS I BRIT GEOG  36 104
   OBUDHO RA  CAH ETUD AF       16  553 76
69 MARKETS W AFRICA
   COHEN M    J TROP GEOG       45   12 77
69 MARKETS W AFRICA STU
   KEIL DE    J ANTHR RES       33  258 77
69 MARKETS W AFRICA  86
   OBUDHO RA  CAH ETUD AF       16  553 76
73 SOAS S
   DERRICK S   AFR AFFAIRS       76  537 77
HODDER E
76 SPATIAL ANALYSIS ARC
   BAKER BL   GEOGR ANAL    B   10   97 78
   CLARK GA   AM ANTIQUIT   B   43  132 78
   FAGAN BM   J INTERD H    B    8  595 78
   GIBB A    TIJD EC SOC   B   69  183 78
   KENNEDY BA  J HIST GEOG   B    4   99 78
   READ DW   AM ANTHROP    B   79  957 77
HODDER J
18 NATIONAL C CHARITIES  117
   SCHLOSSM.S   HARV EDU RE       48   65 78
HODDER WB
69 MARKETS W AFRICA
   BROWN JR    ENVIR PL-A          9 1259 77
HODDERWILLIAMS R
70 J COMMONWEALTH POLIT   8
   BAKER DG   INT REV MOD         5  164 75
HODDES E
72 SLEEP RES   1 152
   REGESTEI.QR  PERSP BIOL        21  232 78
HODEIR A
58 JAZZ ITS EVOLUTION E
   KOFSKY F    J JAZZ STUD        4   11 77
HODEK B
75 ASTHMA BRONCHIALE
   BIRO V    STUD PSYCHO        19  314 77
HODENFIELD C
72 MASS MEDIA FORCES OU
   FREUDIGE.P   SEX ROLES         4   51 78
HODES A
68 DIALOGUE ISHMAEL ISR
   DOWTY A    INT STUD Q    R   22   79 78
68 WIENER LIBRARY B  22   4
   ROSEN SJ   AM POLI SCI       71 1367 77
HODES C
75 BRIT MED J   2 674
   VANDONGE.PW  TROP GEO ME  N   29  374 77
HODES HL
77 AM J DIS CHILD  131 729
   FORBES GB   J AM MED A       239  522 78
HODES R
64 ELECTROEN CLIN NEURO  17 617
   FRIEDMAN S   J NERV MENT      166  110 78
65 ELECTROEN CLIN NEURO  18 239
   TOLAAS J    BIOL PSYCHI       13  135 78
```

38 Sample from the *Social Science Citations Index*

language vocabulary. Because the terminology is that used by the author it will be highly specific and, by definition, a natural language vocabulary is the most specific one possible because there has been no modification of the entry terms by an indexer or information worker. High levels of precision are therefore produced, and with extremely large databases this can be highly effective. The ability to search the databases using sophisticated Boolean logic means that the searcher can manipulate the recall and precision to suit particular needs. However, there is an inherent problem in that if a particular search word has by chance not appeared in either the title or the abstract there is no mechanism for retrieving that item in the way that there might be in a classified arrangement where the search could be broadened further and further using the classmark so that the item is eventually retrieved.

One way around this problem is to make use of a controlled vocabulary in producing the search strategy, and then use that strategy to search a natural-language database. Thus, even though a thesaurus or controlled vocabulary is not used at the indexing stage it can be of great value at the searching stage in allowing users to identify the broader terms and related terms that exist within the discipline and which might have been used by authors in titles and abstracts even if the specific search term has not been used.

Similarly, the problems inherent in natural-language systems over the use of synonyms, where an author uses one particular word and the searcher is looking for another can be overcome by the use of a thesaurus at the searching stage.

SYSTEMS OVERVIEW

From these various strands and themes in the subject approach we can identify an emerging taxonomy or map of the different types of retrieval languages.

There is firstly the differentiation between pre- and post-coordinate indexing systems which shows how the matching process between the search strategy of the user and the strategy of the indexer has been resolved. A second strand is the decision over the control or otherwise of the language or vocabulary of the index itself. This can either be derived from the text through titles or abstracts or it can be assigned through the use of the subject-headings list, thesaurus or classification scheme. These two strands of pre-coordinate or post-coordinate, and assigned or derived term allow us to form a matrix into which we can place our retrieval systems.

	Assigned	Derived
Pre-coordinate		
Post-coordinate		

Into this matrix we can place classification schemes, which make use of a vocabulary which has been structured to ensure that a particular aspect of the retrieval system comes to the fore – namely the ability to identify and make use of the relationships between concepts.

MICROCOMPUTERS AND INFORMATION RETRIEVAL
Microcomputers have had an important effect on information retrieval systems. They developed in the mid-1970s as a way of allowing domestic and small users to have access to simple programming and quantitative devices. They rapidly grew via improved technology and user demand into sophisticated tools that fulfil a wide range of functions within one device. There is now a wide range of microcomputers available on the market, and simple advice and assistance is best obtained from an information unit such as the Library Technology Centre at the Polytechnic of Central London. Consultation with the standard journals such as *Personal Computer World* can give an indication of the range of hardware available.

Cost and software availability are the two most important issues when moving into the microcomputer area and market leaders such as the IBM PC, the Apple IIc or the Apricot from ACT are all extremely valuable within the information unit.

Database-management systems and information-retrieval packages
Database-management systems are software packages that allow large files of information about individual items to be built up and then searched, and particular records retrieved by characteristics

such as price or address. A database in its simplest form consists of a set of records in the same general format that can be manipulated, sorted and printed in various different formats. Because a large database-management program may not leave much storage space for data it is important that the right software package is linked to the needs of the library and the storage abilities of the particular microcomputer being used. All the database-management systems of interest in this area use either floppy disks or, even more relevant to information units, hard Winchester disks that can hold extremely large amounts of information. The hard disk can hold anything from 6 to 25 billion bytes or characters, which makes them very pertinent to the needs of library and information units which tend to be massive users of file storage. At present hard disks are relatively expensive when compared to the few hundred pounds that floppy-disk drives cost, but the costs of hard-disk systems will tumble as technology changes.

The information-retrieval systems that are available for use on microcomputers in information units are essentially modified versions of standard database-management systems. The rather unusual construction of bibliographic and abstract records, with their attached index strings or classmarks mean that database-management systems have to be fairly sophisticated to be relevant to information retrieval in the sense that we mean it. Thus the total file size would have to be at least 5,000 possible items, and the record size, that is the amount of information that can be given for each item in the system, would have to be in the region of 500 to 1,000 characters per record. A basic author and source, along with index strings and a classmark, will use a minimum of 500 characters and the inclusion of reasonable index strings will ensure the record is over 1,000 characters long. Many database-management systems for small micros allow a record size of only some 250 characters, which is insufficient for information handling.

The database would also have to allow searching via inverted files, that is restructuring the database to produce access paths to the item through each term in the index string or through the classmarks or other subject specifier. Thus the information unit has to try to mirror the level of searching strategy that the on-line databases available through host vendors provide. Anything less than post-coordinate searching through inverted files is going to be second best to the user.

This means that the ability to search through the Boolean operators **AND, OR, NOT** is important, as is the ability to truncate search terms and also possibly to browse through the inverted files to see thesaurus links.

Finally the output from a database-management system is important, and information units require the ability to output in different formats of bibliographic record so that various levels of user demand can be satisfied.

Few database-management systems available on microcomputers will satisfy all of these demands, but some come very near. Advances in software design and the increase in the sophisticated demands of users in a wide variety of different commercial areas mean that such packages are becoming more and more relevant to libraries. The world-famous D Base 2 software package is used in a number of information systems, particularly in North America, to run integrated retrieval and library database systems. MDBS (Micro Database Systems) is also a sophisticated and versatile package which can be run on a number of different micros. The speed of change and availability of many of the software packages means that regular scanning of journals such as *Byte*, *Personal Computer World* or *Creative Computing* is essential to keep up to date

Indexing and information retrieval on microcomputers
There are a limited number of programs and packages specifically designed for indexing and information retrieval on microcomputers in library and information units.

Subject-indexing strings, as we saw in an earlier section, are produced by taking index terms from a thesaurus or headings list and then placing them in a particular citation order. NEPHIS (Nested Phrase Indexing System) is a program that produces sets of entries from an input string which runs on a Commodore Pet. There are a number of supporting programs that allow the string to be created and displayed. NEPHIS is a research-based system designed by Professor Timothy Craven at the School of Library and Information Science, University of Western Ontario, Canada, but it is also a system of proven applicability.

Schools Information Retrieval Project (SIR)
The SIR project was funded by the British Library in order to produce a good information-retrieval system for use on micros in

school libraries and resource centres. Originally designed to run on a Research Machine 380Z, it is now available on the BBC B micro. It has taken an extraordinarily long time to move from the original research project to a marketable software package, but it does provide an integrated retrieval system fulfilling many of the criteria mentioned under database-management systems at what is hoped will be a relatively low cost. The system is disc-based for RM380Z and BBC B and further information is available from the British Library, Sheraton House, Sheraton Street, London.

Summary

An enormous amount is happening in the area of microcomputers and library and information-retrieval systems, and full information is often available only through personal contacts and regular scanning of a wide range of fringe journals. Sources of help and assistance include the On-line Information Centre at ASLIB, the Library Technology Centre at the Polytechnic of Central London, the Community Information Project based at Bethnal Green Library, the Computer Development Unit of the London Advice Services Alliance also based at Bethnal Green, and personal contact with library and information units in the field. Journals that are of assistance include *Byte, Personal Computer World, Educational Computing* and *Acorn User.*

The government has also been funding a Micro-electronics in Education Programme which is committed to stimulating and advancing the use of microcomputers in schools. This has resulted in a wide range of expertise in the use of microcomputers in database production, the learning process and the relationship of graphics to text becoming available in schools and area offices of the Micro-electronics in Education Programme (MEP).

7 Management of information-retrieval systems

CHOICE OF SYSTEM

This guide has identified a wide range of possible subject and non-subject retrieval systems, ranging from highly structured classification schemes to ad hoc catchword indexes. Most information units evolved slowly and have adapted indexing languages and retrieval systems that match the needs of their material and their users. However, many information units have to start from scratch and are forced to make decisions on the type of retrieval language and retrieval system that they require.

The choice of a classification scheme or alphabetical approach, pre-coordinate or post-coordinate, controlled vocabulary or natural language, with a manual or computerized system obviously involves a matrix of different alternatives. The manager of an information unit needs to identify key needs and the user is the only salient reference point. The needs of the user group in terms of browsing interaction with an intermediary, specificity of information requirements and ability to articulate need through search terms has to be analysed. Users may require browsing systems because the subject field is difficult to define precisely in subject terms or because the ability to browse stimulates high recall. Alternatively, the user may be able to articulate highly specific search strategies and require a high level of precision in the output necessitating a specific index vocabulary searched either pre- or post-coordinately.

These broad issues can be evaluated, but of course in many information units users' needs are so disparate that a second-best situation has to be adopted, allowing most users what they want most of the time.

An important decision for the information unit is whether to go ahead and design a new vocabulary or classification scheme, with a citation order; or whether to adopt an already existing retrieval language with a pre-determined citation order from some other information unit.

Opinions seems to vary on this issue. In general, very few retrieval systems and indexing vocabularies can be moved from one unit to another. The different users and the different materials within the system mean that if the retrieval system is to be reasonably specific there will have to be modifications to the indexing vocabulary. Those units that have managed to make use of already existing retrieval systems, such as academic and public libraries using the Dewey decimal classification, tend to be acquiring very similar material and satisfying very similar user groups. Students and public-library patrons do not vary greatly between institutions, and the material required in such libraries tends to be mainly similar. Even here, most libraries find that they are making minor modifications to the classification scheme fairly continuously in order to match their particular users or specific material in their system. Nonetheless, many information units feel that it must be more logical to adopt a previously existing vocabulary rather than design their own from scratch. Elizabeth Orna in her valuable tool *Build yourself a thesaurus* makes it clear that she perceives the construction of a thesaurus as a complex task for an information unit. Others, on the other hand, have made clear that the adaptation of a previously existing system is time-consuming and cumbersome and still does not provide the unit with a retrieval system which exactly matches the needs of its users.

The use of an existing language and system is convenient. There are economies in co-operating over keeping the vocabulary up to date and possibly selling the indexing language to other users. The information unit will also receive help and assistance from existing users.

The disadvantage of adopting existing systems is that rarely do users and materials in different systems match. Thus there needs to be considerable modification. Citation orders may not match the needs of the new information unit, and the work required to identify specific index terms to insert into the vocabulary may be quite considerable. However, producing a new indexing vocabulary is a time-consuming operation and it can be intellectually extremely complex. Nonetheless, the process of identifying user needs, citation orders and vocabulary terms can be an important part of the process of planning and developing an information unit.

EVALUATION OF SYSTEMS

Users will continuously evaluate the output from a retrieval system and will respond to their own perceptions of success or failure by either making use of the system in the future or using other alternatives. We have discussed users and non-users and their needs as opposed to their expressed demands. It is not necessarily true to say that if users are satisfied with a retrieval system it must be successful. It could well be that it is the wrong users with the wrong demands who are being satisfied and therefore the retrieval system may not be fulfilling its objectives. An information unit needs to analyse both the benefits and effectiveness of the information-retrieval system.

The **benefits** of a retrieval system are the uses to which the information is put by the recipient. This is the key link which the manager of the information unit needs to identify but it is of course difficult to identify the benefits over long periods of time during which particular individuals gain from a piece of information. When those benefits are transformed into social change it becomes almost absurd to try to make the links back to the original piece of information. However, many information units do feel that their vital social and economic role is ignored because it is not possible to identify these particular links.

The evaluation of the **effectiveness** of an information-retrieval system is a more internal process, linked to the major elements of *cost*, *time* and *quality* of output.

It is important that the manager of the information unit has some conception of the various unit *costs* of all the different parts of the operation, and the total cost of the system in order that it can be judged against alternative systems. Certain costs of retrieval systems are very hidden: the costs of training, learning how to use the system and explanation of the system to users has to be added into the cost of indexing, as does designing and producing the indexing language. Large amounts of time can be spent on cost evaluations and many information units are not able to become involved in detailed analysis.

Searchers' *time* can be expressed in monetary terms. Certain retrieval systems and physical arrangements of material seem to produce answers more rapidly than others. However, the majority of searchers' time is spent on the formulating of the search strategy rather than actually doing the search and thus systems that stimulate browsing and user interaction are effectively allowing the search strategy to be formulated whilst the search is happening. Other systems require the search strategy to be formulated in advance and the search is then done immediately through a database. The relevant time for evaluation is the time between the user's problem being received by the system and a solution being produced. The fact that different systems allow that process to take place in slightly different ways does not affect the time evaluation, although the psychological effect of the time spent interacting with the system may change the user's perception of the effectiveness of the system.

Evaluation of the *quality* of output is the other major effectiveness measure. In the early part of this guide we made clear that the selection and acquisition process had an effect on the coverage and up-to-dateness of the information within the unit. However sophisticated the information-retrieval system, bad input will produce bad output. In many retrieval systems currency and novelty are more important to the user than complete coverage of the subject field. It is the role of the manager of the information unit to ensure that currency and coverage as well as novelty are an integral part of the selection and acquisition process, particularly bearing in mind that the user group will be a subset of the total possible user population and that therefore changes in currency or coverage may widen the market penetration of the information unit into the non-user group.

Recall and precision are two major quality-control measures that relate user satisfaction with specificity of the indexing vocabulary and the exhaustivity of the indexing process. Recall, the percentage of relevant information that the system can retrieve, and precision, the percentage of irrelevant material that the system can screen out, are related to exhaustivity and specificity respectively. Because precision is easy to measure, by taking the output from the particular search and asking the user to judge the percentage of relevant and irrelevant items, it has become a useful measure for evaluating retrieval systems. If a particular search generates 20 items of which 10 are relevant and the remainder are irrelevant then the precision ratio is 50%. Because there is a very generalized inverse relationship between recall and precision it is possible to judge that if precision ratios for all searches are extremely high then the chances are that recall may not be particularly effective.

The aspects of currency, coverage, recall and precision are inter-related in that if the retrieval system is full of dated material then the user will express high levels of dissatisfaction even though the retrieval system may be working effectively. Obsolescent material in the system slows down the retrieval process and reduces precision. Unusual selection policies produce material deemed irrelevant by the user. Thus the evaluation and measurement of the retrieval system must include analysis of the relevance of particular items in the system. In the majority of information units a small hard core of the collection will provide the majority of relevant items that satisfy search strategies. This particular distribution may help to allow information managers to edit and prune their information store ruthlessly, particularly if they are interested in high levels of precision. The obsolescence or redundancy of information in many subject fields takes place extremely rapidly, and this weeding process needs to be a continuous one. Many information units log the items used in response to searches, by marking the actual item so that at the end of a particular timespan those not used can be identified and evaluated for their effectiveness in the total information store. This process needs to be handled with care, bearing in mind the problems of an information unit being forced to specialize more and more in satisfying a smaller and smaller number of highly demanding users.

CONCLUSION
Organizing information within an information-retrieval system is part of an 'information cycle', affected by users, non-users, information producers, the selection of information and the complex role of language in the indexing and searching process. The 'cycle' has several interrelating subsystems that crucially affect each other. This guide has aimed to identify some important parts of those subsystems and show information units how to improve their performance in those areas.

Bibliography

Information users and physical arrangement
Ainley, P and Totterdell, B, *Alternative arrangements: new approaches to public library stock*. London, Association of Assistant Librarians, 1982
Betts, D, 'Reader interest categories in Surrey' in Ainley, P and Totterdell, B *Alternative arrangements: new approaches to public library stock*. London, Association of Assistant Librarians, 1982
Bunch, A, *Basics of information work*. London, Clive Bingley, 1984
Lancaster, F W, *Information retrieval systems: characteristics, testing and evaluation*. 2nd ed. New York, Wiley, 1979
Malley, I, *Basics of information skills teaching*, London, Clive Bingley, 1984

Cataloguing
Anglo-American cataloguing rules. 2nd ed. London, Library Association, 1978
Canadian Library Association, *Non-book materials: the organisation of integrated collections*; compiled by J R Weihs, S Lewis and J Macdonald. Ontario, CLA, 1973
Concise Anglo-American cataloguing rules. London, Library Association, 1981
National Council for Educational Technology, *Non-book materials cataloguing rules*. London, NCET with the Library Association, 1973

Filing
American Library Association, *Rules for filing catalogue cards*. 2nd ed. Chicago, ALA, 1968
British Standards Institution, *Alphabetical arrangements and the filing order of numbers and symbols*. London, BSI, 1985 (BS 1749:1985)

Abstracting
American National Standards Institution, *Standard for writing abstracts*. New York, ANSI, 1971 (ANSI Z39.14 – 1971)
Borko, H and Bernier, C L, *Abstracting concepts and methods*. London, Academic Press, 1975
Maizell, R E et al, *Abstracting scientific and technical literature: an introductory guide and text for scientists, abstractors and management*. New York, Wiley, 1971

The subject approach
Foskett, A C, *The subject approach to information*. 4th ed. London, Bingley, 1982
Lancaster, F W, *Vocabulary control for information retrieval*. Washington, Information Resources Press, 1972
Library Board of Western Australia, *Establishing a local community information service*; compiled by A Keehan and C Riatti. Perth, The Board, 1983
Part I Guidelines for development and maintenance
Part II Subject headings list
Sears list of subject headings. 11th ed. by B M Westby. New York, Wilson, 1982

Classification schemes
The Bliss bibliographic classification. 2nd ed. by J Mills and V Broughton. London, Butterworths, 1977
British Standards Institution, *The Universal decimal classification*. London, BSI, 1961 (BS1000A – 1961)
The Dewey decimal classification. 19th ed. Lake Placid, Forest Press, 1979
Mills, J, *Initial guide to the Universal decimal classification*. London, BSI, 1963 (BS1000C – 1963)

Thesauri
Aitchison, J and Gilchrist, A, *Thesaurus construction: a practical manual*. London, Aslib, 1972
American National Standards Institute, *Guidelines for thesaurus structure, construction and use*. New York, ANSI, 1974 (ANSI 39.19)
British Standards Institution, *Guidelines for the establishment and development of multilingual thesauri*. London, BSI, 1979 (BS 5723: 1979)
International Organisation for Standardisation, *Documentation: guidelines for the establishment and development of monolingual thesauri*. Geneva, ISO, 1974 (ISO 2788, 1974)
Orna, E, *Build yourself a thesaurus: a step by step guide*. Norwich, Running Angel, 1983

Computers and indexing
Armstrong, C J, 'The use of a commercial database management system as a basis for bibliographic information retrieval,' *J Information Science*, 8, 1984, 191–201
Burton, P, *Guide to the use of microcomputers in libraries*. New York, Van Nostrand, 1975
Gates, H, *A directory of library and information retrieval software for microcomputers*. London, Gower, 1985
Hamilton, C (ed), *Text retrieval: a directory of software*. London, Institute of Information Scientists and Gower, 1985

Organizations

Aslib, Association for Information Management, Information House, 26 Boswell Street, London WC1 Tel: 01-430-2671

British Library Research and Development Department, Sheraton House, Sheraton Street, London W1 Tel: 01-636-1544

Community Information Project, Bethnal Green Library, Bethnal Green, London E2 Tel: 01-981-6114

Institute of Information Scientists, 44 Museum Street, London WC1 Tel: 01-831-8003

Library Association, 7 Ridgmount Street, London WC1 Tel: 01-636-7543

Library Technology Centre, 309 Regent Street, London W1 Tel: 01-580-4562

National Association of Citizens' Advice Bureaux Classification Research Project, 115–123 Pentonville Road, London N1 Tel: 01-823-2187

On-Line Information Centre, Information House, 26 Boswell Street, London WC1 Tel: 01-430-2671

Index

HOW TO FIND INFORMATION

in science and technology

Jill Lambert
Peter A Lambert

Because of the immense quantity of new research and other information, the literature of science and technology is formidable in extent. This book has been written as an aid to all who want to find their way through to the information they need with the least fuss, and to those in libraries and information centres whose job it is to help specialists in this daunting task.

The book is of value both to the information professional – by identifying both particular and general information needs and problems as they affect an important category of reader – and to a wide range of scientists and technologists, particularly those entering research and development for the first time.

234 × 156 mm; 112 pp; cased
ISBN 0–85157–394–0

From Library Association Publishing Ltd

HOW TO DO RESEARCH
Second edition

Nick Moore

A new edition of this popular and successful guide for anyone thinking of embarking on a research project.

The book follows the different stages in the research project from the initial idea, through the selection of the best methods, and the preparation of a proposal, to the production of the final report and the dissemination of the findings. The emphasis is on practical advice and guidance.

This new edition has been extensively revised and expanded to take account of current practices, and a bibliography is included.

216 × 138 mm; paper; ISBN 0–85365–787 4